A PLACE OF GROWTH

A PLACE OF GROWTH

Counselling and Pastoral Care
of People with AIDS

ALVIN MARCETTI

and

SHIRLEY LUNN

Foreword by Dame Cicely Saunders OM

DARTON·LONGMAN + TODD

First published in 1993 by
Darton, Longman and Todd Ltd
1 Spencer Court
140–142 Wandsworth High Street
London SW18 4JJ

ISBN 0-232-52025-9

A catalogue record for this book is
available from the British Library

Cover: Illustration by Donald Mullis, based on a tapestry at the
Mildmay Mission Hospital; design by Bet Ayer

Phototypeset by Intype, London
Printed and bound in Great Britain
at the University Press, Cambridge

CONTENTS

FOREWORD

Some years ago Vanderpool* suggested that instead of using the phrase 'dying with dignity' which is so confusingly interpreted with several different meanings, we might find it more accurate and creative to refer to 'dying with a sense of worth'. This book illustrates with a series of compelling stories how this can happen amid the many challenges presented to people dying with AIDS-related diseases.

The modern hospice movement developed from the opportunity to listen to many people who were facing mortal illness, their families and those caring for them. Once the pattern of a specially planned unit with home care and daycare integrating it into the local community and hospital teams was established, it spread both nationwide and world-wide and was interpreted in a variety of ways. The focus on patients with advanced cancer and motor neurone disease enabled a number of clinical and psycho-social research papers to be published and ways of giving support and family care to be defined. The basic principles were then able to make their way gradually into the general field.

When AIDS-related illness began to present as a potentially major problem, this led to the suggestion that this should be seen as a new demand on the existing hospices. However, this failed to note that they were without sufficient beds or home-care staff to meet existing needs, and also lacked knowledge of what new situations beyond their current competence would be presented. Just as the first cancer hospices tackled pain and other symptoms, family needs and openness to a patient's feelings and longings, so a concentration on this

*Y. Vanderpool, 'The ethics of terminal care', *Journal of the American Medical Association*, 239:10 (February, 1978) 850–2.

new challenge was called for. Mildmay AIDS Hospice was set up to take on this commitment and the following chapters show how the interdisciplinary team listened and learned.

The personal worth of often young people facing the untimely end of a difficult life is shown vividly in these pages together with illustrations of the developing confidence and expertise of the team. It is obvious that the approaches learned in the older hospices are being sensitively adapted and developed in this new setting. Some of the demands are formidable but they are presented compassionately and realistically. It is obviously a unit where, as the title suggests, much learning and maturing has taken place on all sides.

It is suggested that the days of such a specialist hospice may be limited and that the general hospices will eventually fill the growing need for this kind of care. Certainly we must all be ready to face new challenges but I doubt very much that such concentrated knowledge will be available for some of the situations so imaginatively faced by the interdisciplinary team at Mildmay. Already, the rest of us are more able to enter this field because of their pioneering work so readily shared with others but the demands of cancer patients are ever increasing, especially for an integrated community and in-patient service. Not only will patients continue to need Mildmay and its fellows, but we shall all help people with HIV/AIDS better if they continue to pioneer and teach us. Just as much that has been learned in the cancer hospices is being increasingly interpreted as the palliative approach in other specialities, so we will all heed and learn from Mildmay. Above all, they have given us a new look at personal worth at the end of life which can make us feel more hopeful about all life.

DAME CICELY SAUNDERS OM
Founder of the modern hospice movement
Chair, St Christopher's Hospice, London

ACKNOWLEDGEMENTS

We wish to thank all those who have lived and worked at Mildmay AIDS Hospice; it has been an honour to be in 'a place of growth' with you. We are especially grateful to Peter Clarke, Senior Chaplain; Dr Veronica Moss, Medical Director; Ruth Sims, Chief Executive; Helen Taylor-Thompson, Chairman of the Board; and Ann Wood, formerly Clinical Nurse Specialist at Mildmay and now Quality Improvement Facilitator at King's College Hospital, London.

1

SHARED BEGINNINGS

It is important that you read this chapter, and this is the reason that it is not called an introduction. Most readers skip them and jump right into the meat of the book, impatient for information and to see what the authors have to say about the subject. This may be especially true with books about AIDS; there is so much to say, and so many people are working in a field which often changes overnight and where there are few guidelines. We feel that what we have to say is important, that it comes from many years of combined experience, and that if we are writing a book then we have the opportunity to guide the reader along the path we want.

The title of this book was inspired by a short story written by one of our patients, and the cover illustration is based on a tapestry worked by another and now hanging in the Mildmay chapel. 'I grew up in such a place' is a line from Robert's story about a family holiday at the seaside. Robert was a uniquely spiritual person, although not a traditional believer in any faith, and he saw his time in the hospice as an opportunity to continue his growth as a person rather than as a time for endings. This idea of continual growth appealed to us as it describes our shared experience in working with people with AIDS (PWAs) and the experience of any number of those we have cared for.

Many who work in the AIDS field find themselves there by chance or circumstance rather than by choice. However, in the past few years many dedicated professionals and volunteers have chosen to make a commitment to the work. For both of us it was a combination of the two: intention and circumstance. We have found ourselves caught up in a some-times unstoppable flow of work at Mildmay AIDS Hospice, and only after almost five years together have we given ourselves the time to stand back and to reflect on that experience. This book grows out of our experience at the Mildmay where I am the Chaplaincy Consultant and Shirley is Head of Patient Counselling and Welfare, but on another level it also grows out of our friendship and personal relationship, and they are both integral to what we have learned about the care and counselling of people with HIV/AIDS.

So our own personal relationship is as important as our professional relationship in AIDS because the one has shaped the other. From a theological point of view this is how some of the best practical theology is done. From Shirley's point of view as a counsellor, it is much the same because the work of counselling people with AIDS is so new that much of the body of counselling knowledge must be used differently in this unique setting. Put quite simply, AIDS and PWAs have changed us as people and as professionals.

It is important that you know us and our journey as professionals and friends so we can share our experience of care in a hospice setting. I came to AIDS in the summer of 1985 when I did a three-month clinical pastoral education course at Bellevue Hospital in New York City as part of my training for the Anglican priesthood. It was there in one of the largest hospitals in the world, and the only one in New York City which takes patients without medical insurance, that I met my first AIDS patients. I came from San Francisco where the media had been running stories about AIDS since the early eighties before we even knew what it was. I knew what the newspapers and magazines told us all: that it was a frightening new uncontrollable virus, that it was confined primarily to gay men, and that it was linked somehow with gay sex. This was a powerful and dangerous mix and one that the less responsible media bit into like a dog with a new bone. At Bellevue in 1985 AIDS patients were barrier nursed, and visiting by the chaplains was discouraged as they insisted that all visitors put on mask, gloves, gown, and shoe covers. I volunteered as part of my training to visit AIDS patients because I wanted to find out more about this unusual new disease and because I wanted to prove to myself that I wasn't afraid. If I could confront AIDS in the hospital, I could confront it in my life experience and the experience of my family and friends in the gay community. The hospital allowed me to do the visiting because they weren't sure what to do with student chaplains, and we were so unimportant to the running of the high-powered, acute medical facility that no one really cared what we did as long as we stayed out of the way of 'real' professionals.

My work with AIDS began with my first visit, and like most of my journey it changed all my preconceived ideas about AIDS and people with AIDS. I donned my mask and gloves, and was ushered into a room where there was a small figure standing up holding on to the safety rails of the bed. He took one look at me and burst into tears and ran to the other end of the bed. That was my first introduction to Jamie. I had read the hospital record card that said that Jamie had been admitted with a diagnosis of what we would now call full-blown AIDS, that he had been to Bellevue many times before, and that he was twenty-eight. What I did not see on the card was that he was twenty-eight months old, not twenty-eight years old! As I said, all my preconceptions about AIDS were shattered; there must be a mistake, children didn't get AIDS. All kinds of bizarre explanations ran through my mind, some so grotesque that I am ashamed now to admit to them.

Well, I can't leave you here wondering what I did in that room dressed like a spaceman with a screaming child cowering at the end of the bed. More out of terror at being discovered by a nurse and reprimanded than out of pastoral technique, I took off my mask, quieted Jamie and invited him to help me take off the rest of the garb so we could play with some of the toys in his bed. It worked; and Jamie saved me from the wrath of the dragon nurses of Bellevue who feel that student chaplains are somewhere on the evolutionary scale between head lice and bedbugs. I stayed with Jamie for a good long while playing with his toy cars and wondering if I could catch anything. I left with two goals clearly in my mind: to find out what was really happening with AIDS care and to get in touch with the fear I was feeling while I played with and then hugged Jamie goodbye. What I did was go to the men's room and wash my hands and face over and over again until I couldn't hold back the tears of fear and loathing for myself and my lack of courage.

The questions raised that day, both about care and about theology, are ones which I am still answering. In many ways the time I spent with Jamie over the summer formed the basis for the style of care I've used since. There was little I could offer Jamie from the traditional pastoral techniques employed by clergy and counsellors alike. We tend towards the cerebral because it allows us to maintain a façade of being in control, of doing something which will make a difference. However, when dealing with children and the terminally ill there is often little that words will accomplish. For Jamie I realised that I could be there, in the room for him, and could relieve for a period of time his isolation. Perhaps I could expand that a bit and bring him out into the world for the kind of physical touch that makes us human.

What I found in that hospital room was a toddler who was losing contact with the world God intended for us all – the love of other human beings. I often describe caring for people with AIDS as standing alongside them on their journey; well, that comes from my experience with Jamie. I literally stood beside him for the three months I was at Bellevue and, with another student chaplain, was able in small ways to bring him back into the world. A gifted group of nurses, who turned out not to be dragon-like after all, co-operated with us in bringing Jamie to the playroom to be with other children. We could stand alongside him to make sure his play with others was 'safe' and when he went back to his bed we could wash each toy he touched with disinfectant. Today those precautions would be seen as paranoid, but there was so much fear about then that people went overboard.

Jamie was not the only patient I spent time with that summer; Bellevue was the hospital where prisoners from Roosevelt Island were taken for treatment, and I had the opportunity to experience my first body search before a visit. Most of these men had become infected through sharing needles and only came to Bellevue when they were very near death. I quickly realised that AIDS patients only came to Bellevue then because they had no other place to go. At that time most members of the gay community were cared for at other hospitals, and there was the beginning of what would become a well-organised network of support. If you had any kind of medical insurance other hospitals would take you, and only the most helpless of cases came to Bellevue. The feelings of helplessness I experienced with Jamie were intensified as I sat by the bed of these dying men, touching, talking, and keeping watch. I began to feel that human beings deserved more than this; that no one deserved to die alone, in so much pain, and in such a state of fear. Their fear was only compounded by the fear and panic of the general public, and I felt that there must be a better, more human, way to die. I realise now that I was preparing myself for hospice work; I was identifying a need from my own experience, and it is ironic that I had to come 5000 miles to London to find the Mildmay model of terminal care.

That was the beginning of the journey which continued that summer at Bellevue and when I came to England to finish my theological training at the University of Durham. I worked with AIDS North in Newcastle which has since become affiliated with Body Positive, and I spent a few weeks at St Oswald's Hospice in Gosforth which was my introduction to modern hospice care.

When I was ordained and came to Stepney, Bishop Jim Thompson and my vicar gave me permission to continue working in the AIDS field, and it was in August 1987 that I began to look around the East End of London for a way to become involved. I did some research and found Mildmay: a redundant NHS hospital which had re-opened as a private charitable trust and would soon provide care for people with AIDS. I learned that it was a Christian evangelical foundation, that a ward of AIDS hospice care was due to open in January 1988, and that the process of recruiting volunteers to work on the AIDS unit when it opened had begun. I wrote and received a polite reply from the hospital director, Ruth Sims, saying that my application would be processed in due time and that if accepted after an interview I would be in the first group to train as ward volunteers.

As I look back from the perspective of four plus years I am amazed that I pursued the contact and that I have persevered given the person I was then. The latter is due in large part to my working relationship with the Mildmay chaplain, Peter Clarke, and what was to become a continuing dialogue of friendship and mutual disclosure with Shirley, my co-author. I come from the Catholic end of the Anglican tradition and while that may seem an unimportant statement to many readers, some will realise that the Evangelicals sit on one end of church pew while the Catholics sit on the other, and there is a huge gap which can never be bridged by incense or happy-clappy hymns. I was suspicious of Evangelicals wanting to convert a very vulnerable population and using hospice care as a medium. I also realised that they would be very suspicious of me, so I decided to insist that I would only work as a practical volunteer on the wards; that the chaplain could mind the spiritual turf as he saw fit.

It was at this point that Shirley, my co-author, crossed paths with me. She has played many roles at Mildmay in addition to the one for which she was appointed, Senior Patient Counsellor, and when we met she was also co-ordinating and training volunteers to work on the wards. Shirley came to Mildmay from community work; for the previous five years she had been a counsellor and family worker with a Church of England clergy team in the Dagenham-Barking area of East London. Her background was in family work, and it was through this experience that bereavement work and care for the dying came to be an interest.

Shirley's husband, Leonard, is an Anglican priest, and when a small hospice was formed in his area he became its chaplain. His work brought Shirley into closer contact with hospice provision, and like me she began to see the difference that it could make in terminal care. Through her own work with families she was able to make comparisons with those who experienced hospice care at St Joseph's Hospice in Hackney and at her local hospice and those who had not. It was a natural outgrowth of working with the dying and the elderly that made Shirley consider hospice counselling when her husband changed jobs in 1987. After a difficult time of trying to commute, maintaining family life, and working full time, she left her job and this coincided with Mildmay's advertisement for a team to set up the HIV/AIDS hospice. Shirley had come from a very evangelical Christian background, but both she and her husband had moved within the tradition to a more central position by this time. Although she was not looking for a specifically church-related position again, the fact that Mildmay did have a Christian foundation was attractive.

In retrospect Shirley can see how naïve she was about working in the AIDS field, about gay life, and about the demands of continuous involvement with a disease of which little was, and still is, known. At the time she applied for the job at the Mildmay, she knew only what an informed reader of the press knew about AIDS. However, she quickly became an 'expert' after a four-day crash course at the local library prior to the interview.

Shirley admits that the interesting thing about the job at the Mildmay was the challenge of setting up counselling services in a new environment and the opportunity to work in a hospice setting rather than with AIDS itself.

Her family was particularly supportive about the prospect of working with people with AIDS (PWAs); however, both AIDS and the groups which were known then as 'high risk' were on the periphery of their family experience. 'We knew gay people, both in and outside the church, but I can't say that I was knowledgeable about gay life-style. I had to find my way in a world which was foreign to me and that was a challenge.' Her first meeting with a PWA was at a training course for HIV/AIDS workers when on the last day one of the trainers asked how many people had met someone who was HIV positive or had AIDS, and then revealed that he was one. This was done to challenge people's preconceptions about PWAs, and however manipulative and questionable the exercise might have been it did begin to bring out Shirley's fears and uncertainties.

It was on her first home visit to a PWA that she began to realise how naïve she was, how inexperienced, and how vulnerable one could be. She went along with a nurse to do a home visit prior to admission and found herself having to take responsibility for the interview as the nurse had no experience in community care. 'It may have been easier for me the first time because I had to carry both of us; Sue was so uneasy and inexperienced at home visits that it fell on my shoulders to appear confident and relaxed.' She found herself

7

talking to one of Mildmay's first patients, John, who was living with his partner and a puppy in a tower block. 'John was covered in sweat and appeared to be quite weak, but he looked nothing like the pictures I had seen of PWAs. He was warm, friendly and attractive and both his partner and sister seemed grateful that we were there to visit and impressed that anyone cared. I found myself worrying more about the puddles of puppy pee on the floor than I did about meeting John.'

However, the fears really began to surface when she encountered her first patient with broken skin lesions. 'I was at St Thomas's visiting a prospective patient when he began to have a nosebleed, and I felt a surge of panic run through me. He really looked like the PWAs pictured in the tabloids, and irrational thoughts ran through my mind – what if ... who knows ... maybe I will get ... what do I do?' However Shirley found that it was impossible to maintain these kinds of fears because of the people she was meeting. 'It was impossible to be frightened of them; they made it all easy for me. I was so impressed with the love and loyalty shown by their families and partners that I was carried along by it until I realised that any fears that I might have experienced initially were gone.'

Unlike me, Shirley had no dramatic initial encounters with PWAs; it was a slow growth of confidence and experience combined with the intensive work of setting up care and counselling provision for a new hospice. It was at this time that the Mildmay care model began to develop and that the interdisciplinary aspect of it was introduced.

As I said earlier, one of Shirley's initial responsibilities was the training and co-ordination of volunteers and I remember one of our first encounters. I had been accepted as a volunteer and was waiting to hear about the training sessions when I got a phone call from Shirley asking me to come in for a chat; there was a patient that she thought I might help with. This was to be the first of many difficult and challenging situations that Shirley would land me in over the next five years. She explained that Leo was causing problems on the ward as he was so demanding that the nurses couldn't deal with others who needed more immediate care. What Leo needed was someone to sit with him, talk if asked to, but mainly to be there and to keep an eye on him so the nurses could have a break from his incessant demands. I don't know why Shirley rang me, whether it was my previous experience or the fact that I was a clergyman, or whether she assumed that a brash American could deal with anything which might come up.

We agreed that I would come in the next day and that if I had anything to discuss afterwards she would be available. The nurses looked relieved when I said Shirley had asked me to visit Leo, and there were some shamefaced smiles as one of them took me to his room. Leo was resting in bed with his eyes closed when I came in; he had that ivory pallor that many terminally ill people exhibit as they near death. He looked to be in his late forties, tall and very thin with the extreme weight and hair loss associated with AIDS. I later learned that he was in his late twenties and that premature ageing also went along with full-blown AIDS. I sat and waited – thought what a doddle, what has Shirley been on about; this man is almost in a coma. Suddenly Leo sat up and began talking, slowly at first, then more quickly, gesturing with his hands and asking to get up, to get a drink, to go to the loo, to visit friends, then he stopped and looked at me. 'Are you my nurse? Can you help me get up please?' Leo tried to move his emaciated body out of the bed, but the drip and morphine driver caught him up, and I thought, 'Oh boy, here we go; what have you got me into, Shirley'.

To use an Americanism, 'It was show time!' Time for me to use the experience I was expected to possess and time for me not to panic. I remembered two things from my time in Bellevue, firstly that to talk was important, not what you said but rather that you talked quietly, reassuringly to an anxious patient, and secondly that touch was five times better than talking, and that combining the two was ten times better than either one alone. So I started a monologue about who I was, what I liked to do, where I was from, and put Leo's hands on my shoulders and held on to his forearms. It worked . . . for about five minutes and then he was off again with his incessant demands and his attempts to get out of bed. This was repeated over and over again; I was supposed

9

to stay for twenty minutes; I stayed an hour and when I left the nurses gave me grateful smiles and tentatively asked when I would come back.

A few days later I was back with Leo, this time in the day room trying to keep him on the couch and off the floor, trying to keep him from changing the television channel every few seconds, and trying to distract him from demanding attention from busy nurses. Shirley came on the ward and we had one of what were to become routine exchanges, 'Ah Alvin, just the man I wanted to see; could you come see me in my office before you leave? I'll leave you and Leo to your TV now.'

Those times in her office after a shift on the ward solidified my education in caring for people with AIDS. I would share what I was doing with specific people, Shirley would comment and get me to explore my feelings. Sometimes she would affirm what I was doing, sometimes just moan with me over a difficult situation, and sometimes offer suggestions for improvement. However, the real learning came when we shared our experiences and admitted our failures, fears, and inadequacies.

'Shirley I feel so useless when I'm with Leo. I don't think he understands a thing I'm saying. Yesterday, I talked and held him for such a long time, and he looked at me so intently that I was sure he knew me and what I was saying. Then I realised that he was just having a bowel movement!'

'Is it so important to you that he recognises you, Alvin? It sounds like you were giving him what was needed, and furthermore you were giving everyone else a much needed break. Be careful of wanting to be "the important person" in Leo's life and death.'

These conversations, out of which grew our working partnership, were not only one way, although I often felt that I was getting more than I was giving. Shirley would ask me questions about male sexuality and about gay life-style that she would hesitate asking elsewhere. Sometimes we just had coffee and talked about ourselves, our families, our personal journeys in life, and our frustrations working within a growing and changing institution like the Mildmay. Shirley became someone I could talk to about my life in the church and someone who could understand the influence of my faith on the work I was doing. Coming from a completely different spiritual tradition, we had a richness on both sides to share with one another and found that we believed much the same things about God, life and death and that those beliefs had been shaped by work with the terminally ill.

One of the important things about working with the terminally ill is that one's theology is quickly brought into focus, and if you aren't sure what you believe you will be compelled to find out very quickly. It is impossible to work with PWAs and not confront spiritual issues. This type of work deals with the larger issues in life and deals with them in a very immediate fashion. There is not time for theological equivocating when someone in the hospice asks you if you believe in heaven or if there is punishment beyond death. However, it is only fair to state the philosophical and theological underpinning of a book like ours at the outset, and we are happy to do this.

We are both committed Christians from mainline, but different, Anglican traditions, Evangelical and Anglo-Catholic. However, in the five years we have worked together and with people with AIDS these labels have fallen by the wayside, and neither of us feel they are any longer descriptive of where we stand theologically or pastorally. Shirley has come to appreciate the healing powers of a sacramental theology, especially confession, communion, and baptism/confirmation while I see much value in the power and comfort of scripture as well as a need for flexible modern approaches to worship and prayer.

What we share is a firm traditional faith in the person of Jesus, the witness of God working in our lives through the quality of our relationships with those we serve and with whom we share love, and the centrality of church tradition as embodied in scripture, the ancient creeds and forms of worship.

What we have come to realise is that the model of caring Jesus gives in the New Testament is still valid today, namely meeting people where they are, instead of expecting them to jump through some theological hoop. We have also widened our view of spirituality and understand that many people meet God in very different ways from ours, but that their experience is no less valid to them.

There are two words which you may well never meet in this book; they are 'love' and 'acceptance'. This is not because we have any difficulty believing in them or that we don't try to live our lives by them, but the words have been over-used by people of faith when talking about AIDS. They have become demeaned so that we can no longer be clear what someone is saying when they talk about loving and accepting people with AIDS. Personally, we feel it is patronising and manipulative. Patronising because it implies that PWAs need our love especially and manipulative because we're afraid it may imply that we feel superior or special because we choose to accept them.

As Christians it goes without saying that we accept those on the margins of society and that it is our special responsibility to be sensitive to their needs and to speak for them when appropriate. It is every Christian's responsibility to care for the hungry, the homeless, and those who are ill, and it should not require any special effort on our part to do these things. We are both working with PWAs because this is where we found ourselves, not because of any special calling from God or out of any desire to accomplish spiritual good works. This book is about the counselling and pastoral care of those terminally ill with AIDS and presents a model of interdisciplinary care which we feel is unique and is worth sharing with others.

We are not being romantic when we say that the last stage of life is a special time which can be used creatively. This time of waiting can be used to repair relationships which have lost their vigour; to evaluate and to explore what has been and to leave something tangible behind; and to deepen or to establish a relationship with God which will continue after death. This is what the last stage of life can be and what is offered to patients in a hospice setting, but no one is required or pressured to take what is on offer. As the person with AIDS waits and is patient, the carer also waits and shares when asked.

2

THE INTERDISCIPLINARY MODEL

Even though the term interdisciplinary care for people with AIDS (PWAs) sounds intimidating and very professionalised, there is something quite natural and ordinary about the concept. In more traditional societies, or even in our own society in the past, interdisciplinary care has been the norm in caring for people with terminal illnesses. Of course it is not called by the same title; perhaps it is just a common sense approach to caring for someone who is at the last stage of life.

In the past it was quite common to see someone who was dying gather an informal interdisciplinary group around to assist with the last things. This group may well have included a doctor and perhaps a person who practised folk medicine, a friend who might offer massage to ease aching muscles, someone who would deal with a will or the parcelling out of the material goods left behind, a cook to provide special foods, and loved ones, especially grandchildren who would visit them. In actuality it is from this traditional base that interdisciplinary care has grown.

Today the last stage of life can vary in length from just a few hours up to several weeks or, in some cases, even months. What we have learned from traditional societies and our own experience is the need for an integration of medical and nursing care with the wider spectrum of patient needs, which may include alternate therapies, spirituality, diet, social and welfare needs, creative expression, and emotional/psychological care.

In England pioneering interdisciplinary work has been done by Dame Cicely Saunders and the team she gathered around her at St Christopher's Hospice in South London.

Over the years the model has been refined and adapted to many institutional situations including the work done in the hospice movement focused directly on AIDS. The interdisciplinary approach is used at the two major AIDS caring units in London, the London Lighthouse and the Mildmay Mission AIDS Hospice. At the Mildmay the counselling and pastoral care components play a unique and important role in the team. Before discussing in detail the components of an AIDS interdisciplinary team, it is necessary to make two important points. The first is that patient care of this type must always be patient-centred and patient-led. The second point is that interdisciplinary teams never truly work unless the doctors on the team are willing to share ultimate responsibility for care decisions equally with the patient and the rest of the team.

Patient-led terminal care means not only that the patient is consulted in developing a care plan or about admission and discharge, but at every step in the care process he or she has the final decision-making power. For instance, when a patient enters the hospice he or she is invited to utilise all members of the interdisciplinary team, to determine the level of pain control, and to make as many of the decisions concerning symptom treatment as wished. There can be no dramatic interventions by doctors, nurses, or other members of the team in patient-led care. In working with PWAs we have found that this type of empowerment is not only appropriate but always contributes to an improved quality of life and often to a prolonged life. On the other hand, no patient is required to participate in the way described, and in fact some are willing to 'leave it to the experts'. Patient-centred care is not without its difficulties and these will be discussed later in this chapter.

The second, and perhaps most important, element determining the success of interdisciplinary care of PWAs is the role of the medical professionals on the team. If the doctors and nurses on the team do not have both a philosophical and political commitment to the concept, the team will never truly function as an effective group. At Mildmay AIDS Hospice from the very beginning Dr Veronica Moss has implemented an interdisciplinary model which values contributions from all members of the team. This is a sensitive subject as doctors, especially, occupy an idealised role in our society. It is the doctor who can make us better if we only listen to him or her and follow his or her instructions. The godlike power of consultants is often not sought but conferred upon them by us, and it is a strong doctor who can resist succumbing to the temptations of power. This is particularly dangerous when dealing with PWAs because the experts have little to offer in the way of treatment. Certainly there is no clear view of a cure or even a vaccine for HIV at present, and the best the medical establishment has to offer is symptom control, treatment of presenting illnesses and advice on prophylaxis such as AZT (Zidovudine and Retrovir), Septrin and Pentamidine. The pressure on the medical professional to assume control is especially great with AIDS because we know so little about the disease, and patients will look to their doctors for relief of both physical and psychological symptoms. However, on an interdisciplinary team which is working well, a key worker will emerge who will have primary responsibility for working with the patient. It may or may not be the doctor, and in our experience it is often the nurse.

Two cases illustrate this situation well, Stephen and Jason. Stephen was a young Canadian professional who chose to remain in England after his AIDS was diagnosed for a variety of reasons, but primarily he wanted to continue working for the international bank where he had been employed for several years. When Stephen entered the hospice he was expected to live only a few weeks, and it was quickly apparent that he was a most difficult person: diffident, angry, patronising, and frightened. He was accustomed to wielding a good deal of power both professionally and financially, and Stephen found it impossible to accept that AIDS would mean a loss of that power. He could finally accept that he was dying, but he would die on his own terms if the interdisciplinary team would allow him. This pushing and testing was typical of Stephen's personality, and one which the hospice team found extremely difficult. Because Stephen had lived his life at the top of the male establishment he wanted to die in the same way, so he would only deal with those he considered to be the 'top man' in each department, ironically those 'top men' turned out to be 'top women'. In the weeks that Stephen was resident in the hospice it was a common practice for the doctor to visit him daily to discuss in minute detail his thrush, Kaposi's sarcoma, or TB. The mastery of the body of knowledge about AIDS was an important factor in Stephen's maintaining his security and in making his preparation for death.

Jason was the opposite of Stephen in almost every way; he was a young man who had been raised by a much loved grandmother, leaving home to follow the fantasy of a career as a disc jockey in Los Angeles and Canada. The reality behind the fantasy was a decade of drug abuse and extreme sexual promiscuity. When Jason came to the hospice he was thirty, but there was an innocent trusting quality about him that won everyone's heart. He would listen to the doctor and his nurse, but how much he took in about his illness he never let on. Certainly he knew he had AIDS and that he was terminally ill, but Jason was much more interested in getting on with living whatever time was left to him. In the hospice he found a love and attention which he had never experienced in his previous life, and he blossomed as he took advantage of counselling, art therapy, the chaplains, and whatever else took his fancy. His nurse took over the medical monitoring of his care, and he accepted without question whatever she thought was best for him. The needs of the two men were quite different, and it was the responsibility of the medical professional to be flexible enough to allow the interdisciplinary team to work.

Once these two major assumptions underlying the success of interdisciplinary working have been agreed upon, then the team can begin to operate. In AIDS hospice care the interdisciplinary team meets at the beginning of each day to discuss new patients and to review the needs of patients currently in the hospice. This team is made up of representatives from what may appear to be a daunting list of specialities; these will include nurses, doctors, the chaplain, physiotherapist, dietitian, counsellor, welfare officer, housekeeper, art therapist, occupational therapist, and volunteers co-ordinator. There also may be input from a masseur, music therapist, and any alternative therapies being employed for specific patients such as aromatherapy, or body work. Patient input is brought to the team by the patient's key worker; as said before this is often his or her nurse, but could be any member of the team.

Each member of the interdisciplinary team will have a unique role to play in accomplishing the objective of offering a comprehensive, individually tailored, palliative care programme. One of the foundations of hospice care is the challenge to see each patient as an individual. The interdisciplinary approach is the response to that desire, and it is in a hospice situation that the person becomes an individual rather than a patient. Then the patient becomes a person with AIDS, a person with dignity and control over his or her life through the use of the model of self-directed care.

It is useful perhaps to expand a bit on the idea of the patient becoming a person in this model of interdisciplinary hospice care. In intensive acute-care hospital situations, which most of our hospice patients have experienced, it is often the illness which is treated in isolation from the person who has it. While acute-care units try to adopt aspects of interdisciplinary care, by their very nature it is not always possible to give the time or the depth required for this model of care.

Because most hospices are private charitable organisations, they are not subject to the governmental and political interventions which have characterised the National Health Service in the last decade. In one sense, it is the hospices who have the luxury of adopting a life-enhancing model of care which takes into consideration the 'full person'. Seeing the patient as a 'full person' will include dealing with both medical needs and emotional and psychological needs as well as those of his or her family, friends, and significant others. Perhaps the best way of understanding this is to take a look at the roles of the members of the interdisciplinary team.

Nursing staff

Each resident in the hospice is assigned a primary nurse who carries the major responsibility for directing their day-to-day physical care. In addition other nurses are assigned to teams directed by primary nurses on a twenty-four hour rota basis. The care provided ranges from traditional nursing care such as feeding, bathing, dressing wounds, medication and symptom control to less customary roles such as providing support for relatives and significant others and acting as a patient advocate. As each resident is housed in a private room, many with *en suite* bathroom facilities, it is the nurse's additional responsibility to integrate the residents into the social activities such as use of the common/day room when mobility is possible. The significant role played by the nursing staff in hospice care cannot be stressed enough as their interaction is on a daily and twenty-four hour basis, and it is usually the nursing staff who are the first to notice any change in a resident's condition.

'I know my patients as people now rather than as cases. At the hospice I have time to consider a variety of care needs in a way I never did when working on an acute-care unit. I also feel that all my talents are used when working on an interdisciplinary team, not just my medical expertise.'

Doctors

The medical experts in the field of AIDS research and care feel that it is inappropriate for the majority of patients requiring palliative, terminal or rehabilitative care to be treated in acute units. The Medical Director of Mildmay AIDS Hospice, Dr Veronica Moss, has pioneered AIDS hospice care in Great Britain and has developed the medical procedures used by a team of junior doctors. The team works on a twenty-four hour, in-house rota seven days a week, monitoring, assessing and initiating treatment, and providing information to patients so they can make informed choices about their treatment. In addition, the doctors attend the daily team meetings as part of the process of determining a care plan for each hospice resident and continuous review of that plan.

The philosophy which underlies AIDS hospice work at Mildmay is set forth sensitively and succinctly in the statement of medical standards:

- Each person is someone of value, being made in the image of God, and should be treated with respect, understanding and acceptance regardless of their ability to respond.

- Each person has the right to independence of choice, and to the information required to make valid choices.
- Each person has physical, emotional, social and spiritual needs, all of which should be addressed when planning total patient care.
- Each person has the right to privacy and confidentiality.
- All who are of importance to the patient should be of importance to us, and therefore our care and support are also available to them.

Chaplain

It is not surprising that an important aspect of care of PWAs is spiritual or pastoral care. It is human nature to question the meaning of life and the possibility of an afterlife when faced with a life-threatening illness. Hospice residents are given the opportunity to choose a representative of their faith tradition for counselling, study or discussion. This is a sensitive area, and while it is our experience that many people come to hospice care as members of the major faiths, there are a significant number who have no belief or no interest in exploring the spiritual dimension of life. Obviously, this desire must be honoured just as a request to see a chaplain would be. Chaplains often take on many roles outside the traditional areas of chaplaincy work. The chaplain in an AIDS hospice is often an agent of reconciliation between the patient and members of the family; this has been especially true with gay PWAs. Chapel services and bedside communions can be very important for Christians, and we have found a consistent demand for sacramental ministry including baptism, confirmation, confession, and anointing. The chaplain's role is one which usually continues well beyond the life span of the hospice patient through the funeral, bereavement work with family, friends and partners, and sometimes ongoing care and befriending of the extended family some of whom may be facing AIDS in the future. It is of primary importance that the hospice patient feels no pressure to deal with spiritual issues or that a particular faith tradition appears to be advocated over another. We have worked with people from all faiths and no faith at all, and it can be said with confidence that those who do choose to explore these important matters have felt a growth in spiritual maturity.

An experienced hospice chaplain says, 'I know it is a cliché but I have learned more about living through working with those facing death, especially people with AIDS. God's time frame is not the same as that of the world, and I have experienced spiritual journeys of importance and depth in the last few weeks of life.'

Physiotherapy

It is often assumed that when a person with AIDS enters a hospice that he or she will be bedridden for the remainder of the stay. However, this is usually not the case; many patients come for respite care or rehabilitation, and physiotherapy can play an important role for these patients as well as for those whose expectation is to remain in the hospice until they die. Physiotherapy in terminal care seeks to enable patients to achieve and maintain their greatest potential and to minimise deficit by using a number of techniques. After an initial assessment of the patient's physical potential, a treatment programme to improve function and motivation is offered. The programme is designed to improve strength and mobility within the constraining features of the patient's illness. For those who will be returning home, a wide range of mobility aids can be made available which will increase comfort and maintain or improve function. These can include walking aids, foot drop splints, wheelchairs and specialised cushions for seating.

The actual physical work prescribed by the physiotherapist has a spin-off effect in that it can improve morale and attitude thereby enabling patients to use the time they have left to them more actively. The approach is holistic, patient-directed and requires close liaison with all other members of the inter-disciplinary team to ensure consistent integrated care.

Occupational therapy

It is easy for the lay person to confuse physiotherapy and occupational therapy or to assume that occupational therapy focuses on recreational skills. A hospice occupational therapist defines her role as follows, 'Occupational therapy looks at occupation; not how to occupy someone, but how each person copes physically with his or her daily occupations (activities) and the effect the "doing" has on one's psychological state, mood, and feelings.' Occupational therapy focuses on assisting the patient to obtain meaning in the here and now. This will help to re-establish the sense of control which can be of prime importance in allowing the patient the freedom to accomplish his or her goals in the last stage of life. The areas of work can include self-feeding, dressing, bathing and toileting, and domestic skills. In addition the occupational therapist will look at the need for any environmental alterations in the home, i.e. ramps, grab rails, showers, raised toilet seats, and encourage the patient to participate in individual and group activities which will increase strength, range of movement, dexterity and self-esteem.

It should be clear by this point that the remit of the occupational therapist can vary widely. Other areas in which work may be done could include relaxation therapy and anxiety management as well as reality orientation. When there is memory loss or confusion the occupational therapist can provide a programme which maintains contact with reality and enables the patient to continue with everyday tasks. As blindness and speech problems can often occur in people with AIDS, the occupational therapist can provide assessment by a speech and language therapist and then implement retraining therapy.

Dietitian

The importance of diet when treating PWAs has long been recognised as an important aspect of maintaining quality of life. The setting of nutritional goals and the planning of routes to achieve these goals is a primary function of the hospice dietitian. Many PWAs will use food supplements to ensure the proper intake of calories while others will have special dietary requirements relating to personal preference or particular food tolerances, i.e. vegetarian diet or soft foods only. Of course in a hospice this is set within the context of the patient's past eating patterns and preferences. The dietitian can also provide education concerning diet especially since some alternative therapies focus on unusual dietary approaches. It is quite possible, and not uncommon, for a patient or a patient's family or significant others to provide some or all of their own catering. A fully equipped kitchen is available in most AIDS hospices, and at Mildmay there is a kitchen on each ward for patient use. This often increases a patient's motivation to eat and to continue good eating habits established at home.

Counselling and welfare

One of the most important and most used services in any AIDS hospice is the counselling and welfare department. The service provided is not just for the hospice resident but will also take in their partners, relatives and friends. Again, counselling/welfare is not forced on hospice residents, but in our experience it is one of the services most often taken up.

A counselling service taking the form of individual counselling sessions and group work when appropriate is offered to both in-patients and day centre users as well as to the extended family of carers in the Mildmay context. Most AIDS hospices have a well-developed counselling service. It is important that hospice counsellors be professionally trained and qualified and that a clear method of counselling approach is understood. It is not so important that each counsellor on the team work with patients in the same manner, but all good counselling must be characterised by an open, accepting attitude to the clientele. Since much of the work will deal with death, pain, anger, sexuality, disease, loneliness, and bereavement, it is of paramount importance that the hospice counsellor be willing to work deeply and often quickly in delicate and painful areas of human experience.

Counselling is understood to be a specialised way of helping people who are being or have been adversely affected by demanding situations arising from personal relationships, major life changes, loss, illness or bereavement. Counselling in a hospice situation can be concerned with addressing and resolving specific problems, making decisions, coping with crises, working through feelings and inner conflict or improving relationships with others.

Hospice counselling will also offer bereavement counselling following the death of a patient which can include one-off sessions or long-term involvement. Bereavement support groups are important and usually run one evening a month for a six-month period. In the Mildmay model all partners of patients who have died at the hospice are invited as are partners of patients who may have died at an acute centre but who are known to the Mildmay community due to a prior admission or other contact. There is no charge for any counselling or welfare service.

The welfare side of the service has a practically oriented, social work remit which can, and does, include a wide variety of functions. These can range from making applications to the DSS for a number of benefits, disability living allowance, or funeral payments to arranging home helps or volunteer support. Many hospice patients arrive with their benefits and housing needs in disarray, and the welfare officer will be called upon to 'sort them out'.

When a hospice patient returns home the welfare officer's role can be important in enabling him or her to live more independently and fully in the community. Transition from hospice to the community or community to the hospice may be difficult for the patient if they are not reassured about consistency and continuation of services. The welfare officer can help smooth that transition.

Art therapy is used in a growing number of hospice situations. It can be an important vehicle for helping PWAs face profound personal crises. Artwork can often express difficulties, issues, contradictions or desires which cannot be easily put into words. Through the use of a variety of materials individuals, groups and couples can explore feelings and create a permanent record of a journey which will become important to its creator. While resident in the hospice PWAs have worked in a range of media including needlepoint, watercolour, and appliqué and the work can fulfil the desire 'to leave something of me behind'.

Other team members

The housekeeper is often overlooked in constructing an inter-disciplinary team, but she or he is responsible for the day-to-day maintenance of the hospice. Patients are also provided with facilities to wash and to iron clothes and are encouraged to make their rooms their own by bringing in possessions, bedding, pictures, etc. from home. Next to the nursing staff the housekeepers are people who provide an important sense of continuity for hospice residents as they will be seen every day while providing practical services. They also help the patient maintain an important link with the everyday world and its concerns. By extension all support staff are included in the interdisciplinary team; this would include maintenance, domestic staff, portering, and secretarial support.

AIDS hospices depend heavily on the time and skills offered by a variety of volunteers who are recruited, inter-viewed, and managed by the Volunteers Co-ordinator. They often become very important to hospice residents for com-pany, running errands, days out, and other small services such as reading, collecting videos, and mailing letters.

This rather daunting team of specialists work with the patient to develop an approach to care while he or she is resident in the hospice and after. However the process begins well before admission when the patient is referred by an acute centre or a general practitioner. Prior to admission the patient is visited by a nurse and told about the hospice while an assessment of his or her needs is made. When the patient is admitted to the hospice, the assessment is presented at the interdisciplinary team meeting where care priorities are deter-mined and individual team specialities are called upon. The doctor and nurse will have discussed with the patient what is offered by the interdisciplinary team and the patient decides what therapies will be used under recommendation by medi-cal and nursing staff.

The following day the patient is visited by prioritised mem-bers of the team, and in consultation with the patient a care plan is written. At this point additional input by other mem-bers of the team is again considered. After the patient has been resident for a week, the care plan is given a formal review by the team; long-term patients are reviewed regularly to consider changes in medication or condition. From the first day discharge is kept on the agenda and discharge planning begins immediately. Discharge is the goal of almost all patients, and it is important for the interdisciplinary team to begin keeping in mind the community-wide demands made by the terminally ill and whether these can be met in individual situations.

Briefly that is how the interdisciplinary model works within an AIDS hospice, but what is missing are the human factors which make the model come alive. There is extensive negotiation between the patient and the interdisciplinary team as to the appropriate level of treatment and pain control and what team specialities are employed. The personalities of all involved are important, and it must be said that a special kind of person chooses to work as part of an interdisciplinary team. Team members must possess the ability to see their speciality as of equal value to others and be the kind of person who can compromise and trust the collective judgement of the team rather than ploughing their own furrow. As said before this can be most challenging for doctors and supervising nurses as well as chaplains and counsellors.

This chapter has described the interdisciplinary team approach to terminal care of PWAs, but it is not the only model of AIDS care. However, we feel that the interdisciplinary approach the most appropriate because it is well suited to a multi-system disease like AIDS. Multi-system diseases can attack many parts of the human body at the same time. The illnesses which PWAs experience do not confine themselves neatly to one part of the body at a time. It is common to have several human systems involved concurrently, such as impaired vision or blindness, mobility, TB in the joints, skin lesions from Kaposi's sarcoma or dermatitis, and bowel problems causing incontinence. AIDS can be compared to a sleeping giant within the body waiting to attack new parts of the human system. It is this dreadful uncertainty which makes AIDS particularly difficult for carers and PWAs alike. It is also quite common to have several life threatening diseases running at the same time, i.e. pneumocystis carinii pneumonia

(PCP), TB, cancer, meningitis, and a patient can come close to death many times before the actual event.

Another difficulty in the treatment of AIDS which makes the interdisciplinary approach valid is that there is no logical progression to the illnesses which PWAs experience. A patient will not move from pneumonia to skin lesions caused by Kaposi's sarcoma to HIV/AIDS-related dementia (HIV encephalopathy); it is more like existing on the edge of an active volcano waiting for the next eruption. The interdisciplinary team is available with the expertise on site to deal with new illnesses or complications as they come along rather than having to wait until someone can be called in.

Finally, it is important to note that our knowledge of AIDS is changing almost daily and we must be alert to new discoveries and developments. One of the most significant developments in the care of terminally ill PWAs is the lengthening time between diagnosis and death over the past decade. This has changed AIDS for many people from a single, acute, terminal illness to a long series of chronic illnesses leading to a terminal stage. What this means in terms of living with AIDS is that we are able through treatment to prolong the life of most PWAs from a few months ten years ago to several years today. This has had a profound impact on the care and treatment given to PWAs, and the interdisciplinary manner of working has proved to be the most flexible and useful in responding to this development.

As committed members of an interdisciplinary care team the authors see clearly the advantages for both patient and team worker to this approach, but the model is not without its shortcomings and problems. Whenever disciplines come into contact there will be inevitable jealousies, conflicts, and misunderstandings. One of the most commonly observed problems experienced by interdisciplinary teams is the overlapping and confusion of roles. The nature of the interdisciplinary team means that boundaries are often unclear as to who is responsible, and the result can be that several people do the same thing or that no one does it. This often comes in the area of counselling and support as many members of the team will see it as part of their responsibility. However, overlap can occur in almost any area. For example, there can be areas of overlap between nursing and physiotherapy in regards to feeding, toileting and dressing; these easily can be seen as complementary rather than conflicting, but conflict can develop in regard to the arranging of home help and district nurses upon discharge. It is important that team members define their roles clearly as an exercise to facilitate working relationships. When this is done conflicts due to overlap are more easily resolved.

Other factors can cause problems on the interdisciplinary team. In terminal care of PWAs it must be acknowledged that there is often an accumulation of sadness which results from the nature of the work. Many of the people being cared for are young and near the age of the members of the team. It is a sad thing to see lives end after only a third of their normal span, and it is almost impossible not to internalise some of the pain and loss. The cyclical nature of the work, with the pattern of admission, treatment, care, and death repeating again and again, contributes to the intensity of these feelings. The result of this accumulation of sadness is often depression and its accompanying symptoms of loss of energy, hopelessness, feeling sad for no reason, and broken sleep patterns. Another result, though often less acknowledged, is anger which is important enough to be discussed separately.

Anger is usually about in some form or another in a hospice care setting, but is not often owned. Angry feelings are natural and are to be expected in a place where people are dying. The problem comes from the way it is handled in a hospice. There is a need to maintain a 'niceness' about the hospice environment which in some ways is quite unnatural and dishonest. Those who work in terminal care of PWAs can feel that it is not appropriate to experience feelings of anger, let alone express them. Anger can develop towards co-workers, at the injustice of the disease and our ability to find a cure, and at patients.

This last is important to take note of as it is easy to fall into the trap of idealising dying people. In fact, popular culture turns out films and television entertainment which do just that. However, those working in terminal care must admit that PWAs who were difficult personalities or experienced problems in socialising before they became ill will continue to have them during their illnesses. The illness may well complicate existing personal problems. Nursing staff find that long-term hospice residents invariably fall into one of three 'D' categories: delightful, difficult, or depressed. As mentioned previously in this chapter, Stephen was a difficult man before he entered the hospice and remained so during his stay which caused many problems with the staff and volunteers. He would ask team members to perform tasks which he knew they could not accomplish to his high standard, then dismiss them with a disappointed expression of thanks. What was the staff member to do with his or her anger and frustration? The answer to this question is that the anger was either internalised or off-loaded onto another staff member or even another staff discipline, only to reappear at team meetings. Team members need to take this into consideration when dealing with conflicts or reviewing team functioning.

There are two remaining problem areas experienced in interdisciplinary work worth discussing: the issue of support and that of competitiveness. In the last five years the idea of support groups has infiltrated hospice care as well as almost all areas of the medical etablishment. Everyone seems to be concerned about the level of support given to individuals and to groups like interdisciplinary teams. The problem comes from the fact that when support is provided, often in the form of a group facilitator or staff counsellor, those for whom it is laid on do not know how to make use of the provision. We all need to feel that someone cares about and values the work we do; no one wants to feel isolated and undervalued. However, it is particularly difficult to provide a level of support for a large team which will meet everyone's needs. It must be accepted by the group that at some point and for varying periods of time, some of the team will feel unsupported. When support is provided, whatever form it may take, it is incumbent upon team members to attempt to make use of the experience rather than constantly looking for another more fulfilling type of support.

The last problem area is a quite sensitive one, and one which many working in the terminal care of PWAs will not want to acknowledge, that of competitiveness. This can take many forms in hospice care, but the most common, in our experience, is the need of staff members to have *the* significant encounter with a patient, the encounter which makes a difference in their living and dying. We must acknowledge that dealing with life and death issues as we are in the care of PWAs is often a dramatic and emotional business. It is quite easy for a team member to be caught up in this drama and want to be centre stage with a patient, especially if the PWA is young and attractive. The need to be important, or perhaps the most important person, can cause problems when working across disciplines. For example, who listens to a patient's expression of their innermost fears, regrets, dreams, desires? The nurse who monitors their health daily, the housekeeper who knows them as a friend, the chaplain who has a direct line to God, the counsellor who is skilled in allowing people space to express feelings, the family who have known them all their life? The answer must always be that the PWA will be allowed to make the choice freely without manipulation, as in all other areas of care.

In conclusion perhaps the best way to illustrate how interdisciplinary hospice care works for people with AIDS is the story of Scottie's experience with the hospice team. His first admission was for respite care in order to give him and his partner a rest and to evaluate his care needs. Scottie lived in North London with William, both of whom were in their late thirties. Scottie had been unwell for a long period and had taken a good deal of time off work from his job as a college porter due to his inability to concentrate and to deal with day-to-day responsibilities. At home he was growing more and more confused and was finding it difficult to take care of himself during the day. When he entered the hospice it was decided that while he was taking a rest he should be assessed by the occupational therapist which resulted in a review of home safety and the installation of rails in the bath. In addition a home help and district nurse were laid on.

Scottie was referred to the physiotherapist as the occupational therapist noticed that he had an odd halting walk, and he was given a series of exercises designed to improve his mobility. Through visits to the counsellor it became apparent that his benefits needed sorting out, and the possibility of applying for early medical retirement was passed on to the hospice welfare officer. The chaplain visited at Scottie's request and found that he and his partner were committed members of a supportive Church of England congregation. Four weeks after admission Scottie went home but was soon back in hospital with PCP.

When he returned to the hospice for convalescent care he had lost a good deal of weight, and the dietitian was called in to plan a weight gain programme. The physiotherapist designed a group of exercises aimed to build strength. During this admission Scottie again spent time with the counsellor discussing family relationships; it was a particular concern of his to decide how much to tell his mother about his illness as she was quite old and living in a convalescent home in Scotland. There were also decisions to be made about how much to tell other members of the family as some of them knew he was gay and some did not. During this stay Scottie made a firm friend of one of the ward housekeepers who was a fellow Scot.

Scottie had been discharged for less than three weeks when the arrangements at home broke down. He was not able to cope with the simplest of household tasks and began leaving pans on the cooker to burn, wandering off into the garden or down the street, and experiencing a good deal of confusion and memory loss. It was a relief to both him and his partner when he returned to the hospice where he would stay for the next five months until his death.

During this time the welfare officer arranged for him to take an early medical retirement package from his work, and family counselling was continued. Scottie went home several times during his last stay for a night at a time and once for a short holiday. The occupational therapist and physiotherapist again spent a good deal of time with him as his mobility was declining rapidly. During the last two months he was often confused and weak and spent much of his time in the hospice day room on the settee watching television, talking with volunteers and the ward housekeeper. Scottie also developed a deep relationship with one of the oldest volunteers at the hospice, a woman in her seventies. Although they had lived quite different lives they had much to offer one another. The volunteer became a constant in Scottie's life, and in many ways took on the role of mother or grandmother in his eyes. This cross-generational support was particularly meaningful to him as his own mother was not able to be with him. Along with his nurse he determined the level of pain control, which increased as he became more withdrawn and childlike.

When Scottie died it was difficult for the team as well as his partner, family, and friends as he had been a resident for so long. His local vicar invited the hospice chaplain and his Anglican colleague to assist at the funeral which was attended by a large number of the interdisciplinary team as a means of saying goodbye to someone who had been a significant part of their lives for the past year. William, Scottie's partner, subsequently attended the bereavement support group offered to him and is currently a volunteer at the hospice.

Briefly this is how the interdisciplinary approach worked for one typical patient, but the example is a good summary of how the interdisciplinary team is able to work flexibly with the needs of individual patients. While we no longer live in a rural traditional society we are still able to take the best of past experience and modify it to meet the needs of today's PWAs. Through the pioneering work of Dame Cicely Saunders at St Christopher's Hospice and Dr Veronica Moss and Ruth Sims, Chief Executive at Mildmay, the terminal care model of a interdisciplinary team working in co-operation with the patient has established the standard for care of terminally ill PWAs.

3

SPECIAL COUNSELLING
CONCERNS

HIV/AIDS has been with us now for over a decade, and we still know very little about how the virus works. What we do know is that the pandemic resulting from the spread of the virus around the world has challenged everyone concerned to develop care techniques which meet the needs of the groups most involved. In this chapter we will look at four major groups which have special counselling concerns as well as make some general statements about specific care issues. The groups discussed will include gay men; families, particularly mothers and children; haemophiliacs; and drug users. Case studies will be used to put the special care concerns into context and to give a human dimension to the complex set of issues surrounding each group.

Before examining how the interdisciplinary model of care addresses groups with special needs and their particular counselling concerns, we would like to begin with some general observations about special care needs of people with HIV/AIDS. In our experience many PWAs have undergone some form of sexual abuse. They carry the shame, guilt, and anger of this abuse and look for understanding and support. In a hospice situation this is willingly given, but there is often not enough time to get into the deep therapy needed to explore fully issues of sexual abuse. Depending on the health status of the hospice resident, there may be only weeks to deal with issues which have been hidden for a lifetime. This can be particularly difficult for counsellors or pastors as they invariably come away from counselling situations like these with a sense of inadequacy. Sometimes the anger and frustration will be overwhelming, both for the counsellor, and the patient as in the case of David. As a young man David joined a men's group with the aim of exploring his sexual identity. He came to the group looking for a safe environment in which to discuss issues which he couldn't face with his family or friends. Soon after he joined the group he was seduced by the group leader, and a few months later found that he was HIV positive. Not only was David's trust broken by the group leader, but his first sexual relationship ended with an HIV diagnosis. When David entered the hospice he was not yet twenty-one and had only a few weeks to live. The hospice counsellor involved was faced with a short time to work through the difficult and complex feelings being expressed by David and found herself overwhelmd by the pain and injustice of the situation. For both counsellor and patient, this was a worthwhile but ultimately unsatisfactory relationship. Given the time frame the counsellor could only begin to scratch the surface of David's grief and sense of loss.

Not all stays in the hospice are as short as David's, and some residents may find themselves with weeks or even months of time awaiting their death. It must be said that dying can be a long and boring process; not all deaths are quick and neat. PWAs need time off from the intensity of the emotions brought up by grief, pain, and loss. Hospice care includes distractions and the normal pleasures of life; the hospice ethos is about living and quality of life. At Mildmay AIDS Hospice early Sunday morning trips to the Columbia Road flower market have become an institution whether the resident is chair-bound or not. Other regular pastimes include trips to the theatre, opera, ballet, and pub outings. The occupational therapist organises concerts through Hospice Arts, an organisation which provides music, drama, clowns, and other entertainment for hospice residents. An important aspect of counselling and continuing therapy in an AIDS hospice will be the regular routine of life, and for those who cannot go out it is important that Christmas and other holiday festivities are brought to them. We cannnot expect terminally ill residents to spend all their time concentrating on serious matters, and a surprising number of people are quite well until close to death.

The last general observation concerns the mental health of PWAs admitted for hospice care. People with a mental illness are not exempt from HIV/AIDS, and we are seeing increasing numbers admitted for hospice care. This creates obvious stress for the staff and other patients, and the question must be asked if hospices are the appropriate place for them, and if not, what are the alternatives? At the same time illness can produce personality changes in emotionally well-balanced people, and this can cause distress for family and friends. It rarely happens that someone becomes more co-operative or pleasant when facing a terminal diagnosis, and it is easy to romanticise dying people. The media do not help, and many people gain their idea of the terminally ill from unrealistic romantic films which centre on beautiful people dying peacefully. In fact, PWAs usually find their other problems are aggravated by AIDS, and that any emotional problems will become intensified. Counsellors and pastors need to understand that care and counselling may be difficult and wearing.

One group which has received a good deal of sympathy in the media are the haemophiliacs who became HIV positive through contaminated blood products in the early 1980s, namely Factor 8 which is used to aid blood clotting and allows haemophiliacs to escape the constant admission to hospital for treatment. Ralph was a chronic haemophiliac who had lived with the disease all his life. Two of his brothers had died from haemophilia as children, and Ralph's life had been a constant battle against the disease which included sometimes weekly admission to hospital. He had married and decided to limit his family to one child, a daughter who is a carrier of the haemophilia gene herself and may pass haemophilia on to her male children. Ralph was fifty-two when he entered the hospice for terminal care and was not expected to live more than a few weeks. Like many AIDS hospice patients this proved not to be true, and Ralph lived at the hospice for several months. When he was admitted both his daughter and wife were prepared for his death, and when this did not happen they found their feelings of guilt and anger very difficult to handle. Part of them wanted the long siege of illnesses to be over and part wanted their husband and father to stay with them as long as possible. One of the counselling issues for this family was the decision about bringing Ralph back to the family for yet another period of time. The daughter expressed her feelings quite clearly, 'I want my dad home, but it's like a hospital when he's here. I can't bring my friends back, let alone tell them why he's so ill. I feel awful about it, but I think it's better for him to stay in the hospice.' Clearly the daughter was preparing herself for the inevitable separation and found it difficult to see-saw back and forth on the fulcrum of Ralph's health status. She also expressed some sadness about having no brothers and sisters with whom to share the frustration and pain, and she talked about the strain on her concerning the need to keep her father's HIV/AIDS status secret. The family had decided that on the whole it was better not to tell everyone due to the possible prejudice the family might experience.

Ralph's wife was also succinct about her feelings; 'I love the man, but I hate AIDS', was how she summed up her attitude. She was particularly angry about the manner in which the family had been informed about Ralph's HIV diagnosis. The couple had attended their regular hospital appointment with Ralph's consultant, and it was normal practice to film the discussion for teaching use. Ralph and his wife agreed again this time, and it was during this session that they were given the HIV diagnosis without any preparation. They had no idea that this was on the agenda and found their shock and pain being filmed for later use. Added to this anger as Ralph's condition worsened was the anger at the number of times Ralph came close to dying and did not, anger at the government wrangling about the financial settlement for haemophiliacs, and anger at the gay community. Her anger at the gay community was resolved while Ralph was in the hospice through her experience of the care given to him by gay nurses. She was able to make good use of one-to-one counselling sessions and explored her past anger at haemophilia for limiting the size of her family and consigning her to an early widowhood. Since the HIV diagnosis she had experienced fear and anger about possible HIV transmission to her, and at times expressed feelings of being overwhelmed by the unfairness of her life.

Ralph stated early on during his time at the hospice that he did not want counselling, that his religious beliefs were enough to sustain him. However during his nine-month stay, he did discuss his anger and fears with the staff, but not in a formal counselling situation. This is one of the true strengths of the interdisciplinary team working model; although all team members have their own areas of expertise, they work in a cross-disciplinary manner which allows the PWA to use team members creatively. Interdisciplinary team working also gives staff an opportunity to utilise their natural gifts for working with people. Ralph developed a strong relationship with the hospice chaplains and was a keen participant in chapel services and ward communions. His faith was a huge support to him as was his church community at home. The fact that all family members shared and valued the same religious beliefs gave them a sense of stability and intimacy that no amount of counselling can bring in a short period of time. The fact that Ralph had suffered from haemophilia all his life also meant that the family was used to dealing with life threatening situations and with the fact that the healthy periods in Ralph's life were a gift to them. Over the long period of time of Ralph's residence in the hospice, the family began to let go of one another, and it was decided that he would not return home, though the family did take two short holiday breaks together before he died. Ralph's wife and daughter lived a good distance from the hospice, and this contributed to the readiness to part with one another. Ralph died with the confidence that his family would be supported by their church community and with a sense of relief that his daughter was given some financial security through the settlement offered by the government.

One of the new developments in HIV/AIDS is that the virus is moving through families with devastating results, both here in the UK and in Africa. Sarah and Michael are a young married couple from Glasgow and have been in and out of hospice care for their AIDS-related illnesses for over a year. Both are drug users and the HIV virus was transmitted to them through the sharing of needles. Michael was diagnosed while serving a sentence in prison for a drug-related crime, and Sarah found out that she was HIV positive during her last pregnancy. They live in council accommodation in West London, and even though they have a history of many years of drug use, the couple have been able to maintain some type of family stability for their three children. Now that Sarah and Michael are quite ill the two older children have gone to live with their paternal grandparents in Glasgow.

Both the hospice counsellor and the Roman Catholic chaplain have spent a great deal of time with the couple, but they find it difficult to do traditional counselling or pastoral care in this situation. Neither Michael nor Sarah seem to be able or willing to concentrate long enough to face the terrible consequences of their situation. Although together they will attempt to talk about the future for their children, after a few minutes of conversation their eyes begin to wander and the concentration cannot be maintained. The grandparents are getting older and wonder if they will be able to face the prospect of raising yet another family. Another important issue for this family is whether or not to test the baby for the HIV virus; he is under fifteen months and still too young for the test to be valid, but they must decide. The baby's HIV status would certainly affect his adoption if that is what the couple decided to do.

In one-to-one counselling Sarah says that she feels that she has wasted her life, but isn't able to make use of the counselling sessions. She does not seem able to recognise the boundaries of the therapeutic situation as other than limits against which to rebel. As Sarah becomes more and more ill, the counselling sessions have become more crisis-oriented which models the way she has lived her life. Sarah is able to deal with an immediate problem then move on to another crisis, but does not allow herself to stop long enough to learn or to examine her journey. In the past few months she has indulged in bargaining, both with God and with reality. She says she has given up injecting drugs and stopped her methadone, and when pressed about this she will say that she doesn't expect to get well, just to get a little more time. She does not allow herself to see the unreal and magical quality to this type of thinking.

Michael seems to demonstrate even less self-perception than his wife, and although he says that he has given up drugs the hospice staff feel that he too is bargaining with reality. While Michael may have given up injecting drugs, the interdisciplinary team feels that he still uses cannabis and pills as a means to cope. In one-to-one counselling Michael tells the chaplain about his strong religious beliefs and the importance of the sacraments of the church while at the same time trying to borrow money. Judgement and punishment play an important role in Michael's spiritual life, and he looks to the chaplain for assurance that he will die in a state of grace. Sarah and Michael arranged several times to have the baby baptised in the hospice chapel, but their chaotic life-style meant that arrangements were made and broken on a number of occasions. Eventually, the baptism did happen, and the couple felt reassured that they were 'doing the right thing' for their child. The chaplain finds it difficult to spend enough time with the couple to develop the depth needed to confront spiritual issues. They want simple traditional answers to complex questions and manipulate the time-frame and counselling situation to obtain them.

Two additional complicating factors mean that counselling and pastoral care for the couple is difficult. As mentioned previously many drug users come from a chaotic life-style where trust and reliability are often sacrificed for immediate gratification. This chaotic life-style usually continues after admission to a hospice until they are immobilised. Hospices have clear rules that no illegal drugs are allowed on the premises and that the consumption of illegal drug while a hospice resident can mean an evaluation of residency. However, as in Sarah and Michael's case, since mobility is not yet a problem, the couple go out at least once a day. It is impossible to guarantee that they do not use drugs while out, so the team must deal with the reality that drug use may well still be occurring. This can influence the entire care plan, and in the case of drugs some users' care plans often end up being reviewed on a daily basis. The other problem is the effect that drug users have on middle-class counsellors and pastors. Drug users may be difficult people to counsel for many of the reasons already mentioned, but they also challenge middle-class conventions and attitudes about what is of value. The HIV/AIDS caring agencies have been slow to respond to the needs of drug users for this reason, and one counsellor states his ambivalence frankly:

I always get a sinking feeling when I hear that we have

admitted a drug-using patient. It sets off all the judgemental aspects of my personality, and I wonder if I will be able to overcome my own prejudices about drug use. The thing that really *gets me* though is that they know that and use my guilt to manipulate me as a counsellor, often unconsciously on their part. Drug-using PWAs are the most difficult and least rewarding part of my work.

It is courageous of this counsellor to admit his prejudices, and this may well be the first step towards effective working with drug users. However, the important thing to keep in mind is that drug use is considered one of the most destructive behaviours in our culture, and as counsellors and pastors we will not be exempt from reacting the same way.

The needs of families have been a thread which runs through the previous two examples, and the story of Leila and her family's needs are the focus on the next story. Leila's story begins in Africa with the tragedy of the Ugandan civil wars during the 1970s and 1980s. Her story is one of continuous loss, grief, and bereavement which is ending with her own death from AIDS-related illnesses. Leila was a young woman when the troubles began in Uganda and she soon lost her father, brother, and husband in the bloody conflict. She left her home country to build a new life in England with her daughter, Melanie. Although she has no family here, Leila feels that the opportunities for Melanie are much greater than they could be back in Uganda. Soon after her arrival she learned that she was HIV positive, and the past few years have seen her health deteriorate to the point that she was admitted to the hospice. Melanie, who is six years old, has been taken into temporary care with a foster family when Leila is too ill to care for her with a view to adoption in the future.

The biggest issue for Leila as she approaches the end of her life is Melanie's future. She is unsure about the prospect of adoption and wonders what kind of family would take the child of a mother who died of an AIDS illness, although Melanie does not carry the HIV virus. At the same time Leila is concerned that Melanie will not remember her and will grow up without any sense of her birth family and her national identity.

Leila is a young woman who is experiencing all the bereavements of a lifetime in a short span of years. For her it has been extremely difficult to grieve for herself and Melanie as she has a tremendous load of unresolved grief in her past. She feels quite alone in England without the traditional support of the African extended family. Due to Leila's shortened life expectancy, the interdisciplinary team have focused the counselling and care for Leila and Melanie in two areas: the future and the past. In one-to-one counselling sessions the chaplain and counsellor have encouraged Leila to explore options for the future and to express her wishes and desires for her daughter. Leila knows the foster family who have taken Melanie and would very much like them to be able to adopt her. She feels that she would be comfortable knowing where Melanie would live and knows that the foster family would be good parents to her. However, there is no guarantee that they would be able to do this.

Leila's other concern is that her daughter should know something about her family and her cultural heritage. She wants Melanie to be adopted by an African family, ideally a Ugandan family, and was looking for ways to leave something of herself behind for her daughter. The counsellor suggested that Leila begin to make a scrapbook about her life with Melanie. This activity has grown into a continuing project for Leila and has been extended to writing letters to her daughter about their life together. As Leila gathers the pictures of her life, both in Uganda and in England, she is beginning to work through some of her accumulation of grief about the loss of her family. As she finishes a section of the scrapbook, Leila is able to share it with her daughter and invite her to contribute as well. The letters to Melanie will let her know some of her mother's personality as they focus of her feelings and the hopes she has for Melanie's life. The important thing for Melanie will be the knowledge that her mother loved her and that she did have a caring family which she lost through circumstance. As the young girl matures these will be invaluable tools in building a stable life in her adopted country without losing her roots in Africa. Leila would like also to leave her daughter some knowledge of the Christian faith which has been a support to her during the tragedies of her life. In the hospice Leila attends weekly communion services and feels that God is with both her and Melanie in the midst of the pain of their confusing life.

While the story of Leila and Melanie may seem particularly tragic and heart-rending, it is by no means uncommon. AIDS hospices are seeing more and more families like this one, and the work done with family groups which have been decimated by the HIV/AIDS virus will become an everyday occurrence. The difficult challenges will centre on the ability of the counsellors and pastors to hold two aspects of the counselling in tension. The grief work for past losses is as important as making plans for the future and leaving something behind for survivors. Using one-to-one counselling sessions in combination with family therapy is a way forward. The advantage of working with families is that there is an eagerness to explore ways to make a positive contribution to the lives of those they leave behind.

Gay men present their own set of unique issues for counsellors and pastors. We realise that there is a temptation to generalise about gay men and want to make it clear that we are speaking from our own experience of working with gay PWAs over many years. Perhaps the one thing that they all have in common is a history of social difficulties, most often stemming from their sexual identity. Gay men often have a good deal of unresolved anger and pain about never having fitted into mainstream heterosexual culture and the resultant sense of being marginalised. Broken relationships with family and former partners is another common characteristic. Robert, the man whose childhood reminiscence gave us the title for this book, shared these characteristics, but in many ways by the time he entered the hospice he had done much of the work around these issues. He was confident and at peace with himself about many things, but soon after he entered the hospice he requested to see a counsellor. At the first session he was able to state clearly the issues on which he wanted to work and gave a lucid description of his past. Robert had worked at many jobs in his life, but all had been in the creative end of the media. His work had taken him all

41

around the world, and this travel, combined with living in foreign countries for long periods of time, gave him the freedom to explore and to come to terms with his sexuality. Although he had never had a partner for a long period of time, he did develop lasting relationships which began as sexual and then moved to friendship. Robert was quite close to his brother and relations with his parents had been good, partially due to the fact that he spent much of his time abroad.

When Robert came to the hospice he had been enduring a long siege of illnesses and had experienced a tremendous weight loss. He had an extremely fragile and wasted appearance, nothing like the robust man of forty pictured in the album he showed to visitors. Robert was unusual in that he could identify the issues he wanted to confront, and it is not surprising that he had left them to the last. A few years previously, his parents had both committed suicide together. The feelings of despair and confusion had never left him, and he very much wanted to see some meaning to his life and to search for a reason to continue living. Needless to say the counsellor was surprised when Robert said, 'I want to cry for my parents; I haven't done that and I think I need to before I die.' It isn't often that we are presented with such a clear agenda from someone so ill.

It was not difficult to set boundaries or a contract with someone like Robert. In our experience, we find that many gay men are quite good about delineating which areas need work, and these invariably have something to do with past relationships. With Robert it was the relationship with his parents, but it could have been past partners, siblings, or friends. Often gay men will want to contact a past partner who has been particularly central to their lives, 'the love of my life', and to see them again before they die. It is not uncommon for past partners to become primary carers, or even ex-wives for that matter. The issue of gay men who have been married is more common than some believe and is dealt with elsewhere in this book. Like many gay men, Robert liked tidy endings and he decided for himself when his counselling was concluded. Robert's counsellor realised that they both needed her to continue to visit when he fell quite ill and was unconscious. It is quite important to note that in hospice work the commitment of the counsellor, pastor, and other team members does not stop when the specific contract of work is completed. Counsellor and pastors especially feel the need to follow PWAs through their last illnesses and to be there for the survivors as well. The nature of terminal work requires a quite flexible contract which often demands intensive input over a short period of time. One of the challenges of the work is maintaining professional distance and boundaries while working deeply at the last stages of life.

Robert stated very clearly that he did not believe in an afterlife but was not opposed to seeing a chaplain. In fact the Anglican chaplain spent a good deal of time with him discussing spiritual issues. 'I found Robert a deeply spiritual man but not in any traditional sense. He drew great strength from nature and his writing showed that he saw God present in all his creation. Robert often said he saw no reason for going to church as life itself was an act of worship to our creator. I found it difficult to disagree with him in many ways.' The chaplain continued to visit Robert until he died. During his last illness the chaplain spent a good deal of time sitting with him, holding his hand, and not demanding conversation when Robert was too weak to speak.

Perhaps it would be appropriate to close this chapter with a short reminiscence written by Robert just before he died. As he was sorting out his household belongings prior to entering the hospice he came across several sets of napkins which he decided to send off to friends as something to remember him by. It expressed his pleasure in the little things which make up our lives and at the same time expressed a common desire to leave something of ourselves behind.

> Yesterday I ironed two sets of napkins, lovingly and with sadness. I was preparing for our separation – the napkins and I. One set was bought in Hong Kong in a Chinese Government Emporium. The handwork had been patiently done by some anonymous lady in who-knows-what corner of that enormous land for a few pennies . . . slightly less than the low price I paid. The size of the napkins (large and practical) and the rose-buds appliquéd on each corner endeared them to me

twenty-five years ago, a pleasure which never waned. Rude guests would sometimes leave wilful stains on my beautiful Chinese napkins, forcing me to apply bleach with trepidation. But they all survived . . . *have* survived me . . . and will survive *me*. I must fold them and place them in a bag, to be packed . . .

The second set feels like heavy lace. Dyed a magnificent scarlet they have brightened many a supper table and made an occasion feel special. [Sarah's] mother, from Argentina, left them as a house gift after staying with me for a week in 1970 . . .

During my childhood our home was frequently upset by my mother's illness or absence. When anyone visited there had to be wild hunts for towels, tableclothes and clothes in drawers, cupboards and laundry baskets. Nothing was orderly . . . chaos was the norm. Other homes had neat piles of things that had been washed and folded and put away. Occasionally I would be invited to a meal and be given real, cloth napkins. Such luxury! Thereafter, the only way to measure the validity of a meal was by the presence of REAL napkins. From then on . . . gracious living meant providing real, cloth napkins with a meal – no matter how humble the fare. I aspired to have several sets of napkins in case there was no time to launder them between meals. Such bliss to drop soiled napkins into the laundry basket knowing there were more in the drawer.

It pleases me to think my napkins will continue to grace tables and enhance gatherings of people who will talk and laugh and – perhaps as they fold their napkins to leave the table – remember me.

4

CARE AND COUNSELLING ISSUES

One of the most interesting aspects of the counselling and pastoral care of PWAs is the unique challenge presented. Each day is full of surprises, some quite pleasant and others much more difficult. There is an uncertainty to how the presenting illnesses progress and the unexpected is more the norm than not. While accepted counselling and pastoral care techniques which focus on talking through feelings and problems are commonly used, the care giver must be prepared to be creative and to search out new approaches. This chapter will discuss the important issues which are unique to HIV/AIDS and will explain how experience has shaped our practice in counselling PWAs.

One of the first residents in the Mildmay AIDS Hospice gives a clear picture of the uncertain and unique nature of the work. Mark was living in a high-rise flat with a friend and was recovering from pneumonia, PCP, when he was visited by a counsellor from the hospice with a view to admitting him for a period of respite care. Though sparsely furnished the flat was clean, and it was obvious that Mark was well looked after by his friend Robert. He had the wasted appearance which is typical of many PWAs especially in the later stages of illnesses, and he was quite weak from the pneumonia. It was thought by the senior nurse who accompanied the counsellor on the visit that Mark might well be terminal. His only hesitation about coming to the hospice was that he would be one of the first residents and didn't know what to expect. Mark, who was thirty-five, explained that he was a gay man who had worked in the theatre before he fell ill and that his goal while at the hospice was to be able to walk again. He also explained that he had been raised in a traditional

Roman Catholic family and had left his home country to escape small town life. After admission and a stay of about five days, he gained a good deal of strength and was able to return home. He left the hospice feeling that he would continue to improve, and everyone felt that he might expect a long period of better health.

Within three months Mark was readmitted to the hospice after suffering another bout of PCP. He was to stay there for the next five months until he died, and it was at this time that the layers of his life began to unfold and the complex of problems was revealed. In conversations with the counsellor, Mark affirmed that he was a gay man but that he had been married and had three children whom he loved and had supported since his separation eight years before. His ex-wife lived in the north of England with the children, and their relationship appeared to be full of unresolved anger and guilt. Mark very much wanted to see his children as he came closer to the end of his life. His ex-wife reluctantly agreed but insisted that all evidence that the hospice was an AIDS hospice be kept from the children and that none of the staff speak to them during the visit. He continued to receive support from his friends, especially Robert who visited regularly and even brought Mark's much loved dog several times.

Near the end of the year Mark died in the hospice and though there was no money for the elaborate funeral he had planned, the hospice arranged for the mass and funeral services with financial aid from Frontliners, CRUSAID, Quest, ACET, and the Terrence Higgins Trust.

The work done with Mark, his family and friends is typical in many ways of the challenges spoken of earlier and gives us an opportunity to look at some of the important care and counselling issues. There was an exceptional amount of anger around for all the people concerned. Mark's ex-wife was very bitter about his homosexuality; they had married when they were both teenagers facing an unwanted pregnancy. Mark explained that he always knew he was gay, hated the idea, and married as a means of escape from his guilty feelings. After three children and eight years of marriage, he left his family to live as a gay man. His ex-wife was not able to come to terms with her feelings of betrayal and abandonment and was unable to take advantage of any counselling offered by the hospice. She was trapped inside her understandable feelings of anger and bitterness. Mark's anger took the form of self-hatred and frustration at not being able to see his children or tell them the truth. Some staff became angry at the conditions set by Mark's wife for the visits by his children, feeling that it was unfair of her to shield them from the truth and to require the hospice to remain at arm's length. However they felt bound to respect her decision as did Mark. During his stay in the hospice, the interdisciplinary team meeting often was dominated by these angry feelings, and the counselling staff provided an important group facilitation role. Mark's friend, Robert, shared this anger and spent many hours with the hospice counsellor dealing with this.

Related to these feelings was the issue of guilt, especially on Mark's part. Knowing he would die soon, Mark experienced guilty feelings about leaving his children without adequate financial support, as well as without a father. His feelings of guilt also focused on his sexuality, and it was obvious that even though he had been actively gay for fifteen years he had not accepted his sexuality as a positive personality element. This sexual guilt influenced his spirituality, and he was positive that he would be punished in the next life. He believed in purgatory and that his soul would remain there to be cleansed before entering heaven and found it almost impossible to accept other interpretations. An interesting manifestation of this religious guilt was Mark's ambivalence towards the three Roman Catholic chaplains who visited him. He felt most comfortable with the traditional conservative priest who brought him communion twice a week, but at the same time could not discuss his guilty feelings with him. He did speak deeply, and at length, with a younger liberal priest who worked in secular ministry and dressed in casual clothes, but there he found it difficult to believe him because Father Tim 'did not look like a priest'. Eventually Mark found a spiritual companion in the form of Sister Anna, a Roman Catholic nun, with whom he could explore his profound sense of guilt and punishment.

Surrounding these other feelings and providing a theme which penetrated them all were Mark's fears and sense of loss. He was plagued by a dreamlike image which would appear to him at the doorway to his bathroom or at the foot of his bed. The figure was always dressed in a short Roman toga and beckoned him to follow. Mark's fear was that if he did follow the spectre then he would die. The interdisciplinary team interpreted this as a form of mild dementia and worked with Mark using relaxation techniques to reduce the anxiety he felt. He also was plagued by the fear of punishment by God as mentioned previously and by the fear that he would never resolve the relationship with his ex-wife. In fact, he was not able to resolve this last fear due to his ex-wife's physical and emotional distance.

Mark was a young man who was facing the loss of everything he had valued in his life. Not only his family and children but the active and busy life he had led at work were all coming to an end for him, and this was difficult to accept. He did have the advantage of time in the hospice to talk with his counsellor and work towards his death. An important means to accomplishing this was the working through of unresolved feelings and desires. His sense of power and control over his life was emphasised by the time he spent arranging the visits by his children and the format for his funeral. However, Mark was never really able to accept his physical diminishment and disfiguring. He had been a handsome man with boyish good looks and genuine charm which had made him very successful in the gay pub scene in which he chose to socialise. His weight loss, being confined to a wheelchair for many months, and skin problems made him almost unrecognisable to those who had known him before. Obviously a great deal of his sense of personal worth was bound up in his physical appearance, and the interdisciplinary team made slow progress in moving him towards accepting the other more permanent and meaningful aspects of his personality. Certainly he had not lost his ability to charm, and he was a great favourite among the nursing and support staff in the hospice.

Mark ended his life on a very mixed note. He felt that he had resolved many of his feelings of anger and guilt, and the planning of his funeral and the visits by his children restored some of his sense of control and power. Whether or not he died believing that he would be punished by God is not known, but he did receive the last rites and the funeral mass he had requested. The funeral was an important ritual occasion for Mark's friends and the team. He was loved and a lovable person, and it is always hard to lose someone who has been a long-term hospice resident. The funeral played an important therapeutic role in the grieving process. Everyone agreed the service was just as Mark had wanted, 'camp and over the top'. The sad note in Mark's final song was that his ex-wife would not allow the children to attend the funeral.

It is important to present the complex and many layered story of Mark's relationship with his family, friends, and the interdisciplinary team as it elucidates the complex nature of working with PWAs in an hospice setting. Moving toward the goal of treating Mark as a person with continuing needs, both physical and emotional, was not an easy process. Each week brought new challenges and demanded concentration and creativity by all concerned. This story is probably more typical than not.

As we discuss the important issues which are unique to working with PWAs, examples from our experience will be used. Often only part of a much longer case history will be given for the sake of brevity, but there is always much more which could be said. The major areas covered in this chapter will focus on the many aspects of fear experienced by PWAs in a hospice setting, anger which is an aspect of all illness but particularly in HIV/AIDS, issues of loss and guilt, and finally death and spirituality. These form, in our opinion and experience, a complex of issues which have unique manifestations when counselling and caring for PWAs.

There are many fears unique to HIV/AIDS, but perhaps one of the most compelling is the fear of HIV/AIDS-related dementia, also known as HIV-related brain impairment. It is very much like senile dementia, but it stands out when experienced by a young person. One of the most difficult aspects of AIDS-related dementia is that it can be selective and transitory. It is quite common for the dementia to come and go, and there will be times when the patient will be aware and fearful of another onset. This was the case with Gary who was a young man of thirty-three when he came into the hospice for terminal care. When he was experiencing periods of dementia he would confuse his physical surroundings, forgetting what to do next after he had raised a spoon to his mouth. It was particularly difficult in the hospice day room as Gary would get up from his chair for a cup of tea, forget why he had stood up, then sit down without remembering where the chair was located and end up on the floor with a sheepish grin on his face. Another form can be when an entire section of one's life is forgotten while everything else is retained. One hospice resident spoke about being afraid to go for walks as he might meet someone he had forgotten. He remembered his childhood and early days well and could hold on to the present, but the recent past was a blank for him. This resulted in anxiety attacks when he went out in public, and he eventually became more and more reclusive.

Currently, those working in the field are seeing more dementia, but it is not as severe as that seen previously. This is due mainly to better treatment and therapy. The interdisciplinary team approach to dealing with HIV/AIDS dementia offers a surprisingly wide range of therapies, especially since it is difficult to enter into a counselling relationship with someone who is experiencing dementia. Since we are seeing much less severe manifestations of dementia, it is quite common for the occupational therapist to introduce simple relaxation techniques to deal with anxiety. Breathing control exercises, relaxation tapes, and guided visualisations can create a calm, stress-free environment. It is also important that carers do not assume that someone experiencing dementia can't continue normal functions under supervision. Chaplains find that most want to continue receiving visits and communion on a regular basis if that has been their previous pattern. Often PWAs experiencing dementia will be well enough otherwise to return home or to sheltered accommodation. The welfare officer can arrange discharge to a safe, caring environment where they will receive support and their safety will be of prime concern.

A pioneering example of this type of residential accommodation is Patrick House located in the Borough of Hammersmith and Fulham in West London. Opening in the spring of 1992, Patrick House is Britain's first twenty-four hour residential care service for people with HIV-related brain impairment who are no longer able to live alone, or whose careers can no longer cope due to the effects of HIV on their mental health. Patrick House is part of the St Mungo Community Trust and is managed by the FLAGS organisation; they provide interdisciplinary care for four PWAs. At the time of writing Patrick House is the only such facility, and there is a need to expand this type of provision as the HIV/AIDS community grows.

Perhaps one of the most distressing fears faced by PWAs is the change in body image. In our society a great deal of our sense of personal worth is determined by how we perceive our physical appearance. We are constantly bombarded by the media, and especially advertising, to maintain a fit and youthful appearance, and the young are particularly vulnerable. In the gay community there has always been an emphasis on youth and beauty, and all PWAs are challenged by the dramatic body changes which occur due to AIDS-related illnesses and the subsequent loss of sexual attractiveness. We have mentioned wasting and premature ageing in the case of Mark and the feelings he experienced. It is possible to encourage weight gain, and the dietitian plays an important role in proper nutrition and in developing a diet which is high in calorie intake. An obvious, but often neglected therapy, is encouraging the person with AIDS to choose clothing which fits and to some extent can disguise their weight loss. It is common for the patient to continue wearing the same clothing throughout their illness even though they may have lost 30 or 40 pounds. Fashionable, well-fitted clothes can make a dramatic and positive change in attitude.

Another typical change in body image is the onset of Kaposi's sarcoma, or KS, which can appear on the face, hands, and upper body as well as other places on the body and internally. Removal of the dark purple lesions is not always advisable, and often the patient must cope with the disfigurement. Until recently conventional wisdom declared that only gay men experienced KS, but that has proven not to be the case. Hospices are now beginning to see women with KS.

The families and partners of PWAs experiencing changes in body image benefit from counselling which focuses on staying in touch with the person they knew before the illness changed them. Discussing family histories, keeping photographs of their loved one as he or she appeared before, and talking about the feelings they are experiencing are important. This helps to create a sense of the person they love and an ability to accept the value of what remains. Patients themselves can be introduced to the use of camouflage make-up to hide the KS lesions and when this is combined with counselling an accommodation with the situation can come about.

Women can experience these problems; however, the most common body image problem for women, after wasting and premature ageing, is cervical bleeding which causes discomfort and anxiety about moving around. This can be treated with medication, but the medication can produce a bulbous stomach and sometimes the appearance of pregnancy. Art therapy can be especially useful in releasing the pain and distress of a changed body image for both women and men. Since it is not a talking therapy, PWAs are often able to access feelings which they would be hesitant to verbalise and to get in touch with the profound emotional implications of changing health and increasing disability.

Fears around changes in body image are often very difficult for the counsellor, and it is important that these fears are taken seriously. The unusual aspect of this for the counsellor is that he or she is actually seeing the cause of the emotional pain rather than just hearing about it. The work in this situation is much like dealing with a bereavement, and this is useful to keep in mind when counselling families and partners. They, too, are suffering a loss and often can't imagine making love to the person or even touching them. In situations where the partners may be HIV positive also, it is particularly painful for them because they are seeing in their loved one what they may be experiencing soon.

The use of touch is also important when dealing with body image problems. It is important that the care giver not be afraid to touch if it seems appropriate. This seems particularly useful for chaplains who come from a Christian tradition which includes holding hands while praying, and the laying on of hands for prayers, healing, blessing, or pronouncing blessings after confession and absolution. A hospice chaplain says:

> I never insist on touching, but I simply offer to hold hands during prayer or indicate that I would like to place my hand on a patient's head while giving a blessing. In my experience, this often has been the beginning act of trust. We 'talk at' people so much of the time that it is a special gift to offer silence and touch within the context of prayer. I think the children with AIDS that I've worked with taught me an important lesson because I couldn't use my usual bag of verbal tricks on them. What I could do was hold them and offer my own prayers silently. Adults need that too.

Another common fear shared among PWAs is the fear of a premature death. Accepting death is not an easy process for anyone, but it is particularly difficult at a young age when others can expect to live another thirty or forty years. The inevitable 'why?' questions arise and there are no easy answers. In the past decade there has been a great deal written about death and bereavement, and the so-called stages of grieving are commonly accepted in the care of the terminally ill. However, in our experience, we find this progress from despair to acceptance a bit artificial. Expectations of acceptance often meet the needs of the health care professional and give them a feeling of accomplishment, but the question must be asked, 'Does this model actually represent the experience of dying people, especially PWAs?'

Our answer is that we have seen much more resignation among the young people in AIDS hospice care. Accepting the loss of a life of potential and coming to terms with a shortened life span is not an easy task and those giving care to PWAs must keep in mind that it is not appropriate to force an outside model of grief onto patients. This was clearly the case with François who was twenty-five and had just completed a degree in French at a large Midlands university. A few months before graduation he learned that he was HIV positive, and he soon became ill with AIDS-related illnesses. François was an only child whose mother had died a few years before, and he carried the extra burden of knowing that his middle-aged father would be left alone. Through traditional counselling methods, François was able to accept that his sexual experimentation at university had resulted in his HIV status, but he could never accept that this was 'fair' or to truly ready himself for death. In our experience some young people have an easier time of accepting death than middle-aged PWAs; François had every reason in the world to be angry, to feel cheated, and to rage against the unfairness of life.

This example brings up the problem of the parents and siblings who face fears of their own. It is not a natural event for a child to die before its parent, and the traditional parent/child relationship is violated. In our culture fathers are expected to care for and to protect their children, and the feelings of impotence can be overwhelming when a child dies young. Some of the best therapeutic situations for parents occur on a casual basis in the hospice. Day-to-day contact with other parents in the hospice day room, and the support which can be drawn from shared experiences, bring a healing and acceptance which can take months in individual therapy. Many parents and siblings do not have months to come to terms with the issues, and it is not unusual for parents to learn that their child has AIDS, is gay or a drug user, and is dying, all in one day. One Christmas three mothers spent the holidays together at the Mildmay nursing their sons and drawing strength from one another as they exchanged stories about their sons' lives. Rather than intervene in what became a very therapeutic relationship for the three women, the staff restrained their desires to offer professional advice and allowed the mothers to set their own support agendas. Sometimes doing nothing is the best we have to offer. After the death has occurred, family support and bereavement groups offered by most hospices also play an important role in coming to terms with the death of a child.

Unresolved relationships present another category of fears experienced by PWAs; the obvious focus of the fears being that the relationships may never be resolved. Past partners, parents, and family concerns make up the main body of these relationships, and care and counselling aims towards some resolution of the conflicts. A surprising number of gay men have been married, and there may well be children as well as an ex-wife still in the picture. The welfare officer is often the member of the interdisciplinary team who takes on the job of finding family members with whom the patient has lost touch. Many times the family members or past partners will renew their relationship with the person with AIDS, and it is not uncommon for ex-wives to play a central caring role. It is important in one-to-one counselling that the PWA be given plenty of time to explore the feelings left with them from past relationships. The counsellor needs to be sensitive to timing the suggestion that the past can be redeemed in some measure by dealing with it in the present. From this point, renewing of contact can be suggested and pursued if appropriate.

Counsellors offer family therapy, and a large number of PWAs will take advantage of this hospice service. Two counsellors are often used to bring family members together for group work and to introduce the gay partner into the dynamic if possible. This can be a volatile situation, and violent behaviour on the part of family members does occur at times. We have found that it is often brothers who cannot accept their sibling's gay life-style or partner. If this is the case, the counsellors can then institute a timetable for visiting to avoid further conflicts. It should be stressed that counselling and support is available to all family members and to the extended family as well. As mentioned previously the interaction between families can be important; the mothers who spent Christmas together in the hospice nursing their sons is a good example of this learning from other family models. The casual, non-institutional atmosphere of most hospices encourage this important interaction.

Parents may well feel rejected or deceived by their children if the PWA has not revealed their health status to them before entering the hospice. This is true with drug users as well as gay men. The families of drug users often speak of the double shame: drug use and AIDS. Many gay men move away from their families and remain distant emotionally because they cannot discuss their sexuality; this is especially true of older gay men who were raised in the less permissive 1940s and 1950s. If this is the case, the interdisciplinary team needs to be aware that the best entry into the family dynamic is often through a female member, and sisters can often play a bridging or negotiating role in family counselling. Chaplains also find themselves cast in this bridging role, especially if the family has religious concerns about judgement from God. In this situation a bedside communion can operate as a service of reconciliation or as an agent for the PWA to reclaim his or her family's faith. The chaplain can also play a key role in modelling non-judgemental acceptance of the PWA, thereby giving the family permission to do likewise. Family therapy which involves all family members is also useful with haemophiliacs as their families are often more close-knit than others. Haemophilia is a family disease and AIDS often becomes a family disease as well. In some ways they are more used to dealing with illness and adversity, and they come to counselling with more resources than those families for which terminal illness is something new.

Anger is a pervading theme which occurs throughout any terminal illness, and PWAs are no exception. It is easy for a counsellor who is physically healthy to encourage acceptance of the losses presented by illness and to subtly manipulate towards this end. The counsellor and other members of the interdisciplinary team need to take the loss of choices experienced by PWAs, and the subsequent anger, seriously. How we deal with these issues will establish the level of trust in the counselling relationship and will set the scene for dealing with even bigger issues. The authors want to stress that the loss of choices can be a greater trauma than the HIV diagnosis itself. It may take longer to accept these losses than to accept actual presenting illnesses. PWAs can often feel quite well, but due to the unpredictability of the AIDS illnesses they must be careful about the choices they make.

In many ways haemophiliacs have already experienced a life of limited choices. Job choice, parenthood, mobility and even marriage are all affected by this disease, and sufferers have had a lifetime to come to terms with loss of choices. However, this experience does not diminish the pain of accepting an HIV diagnosis, and their anger often focuses on the 'why me?' questions. Gay men also face a continued life of limited scope. There often is a good deal of anger around relinquishing an active life and accepting that while everyone else gets on with life the person with AIDS must face important decisions at a much earlier stage in life. Career prospects, travel, living accommodation and the loss of a gay life-style are usually difficult issues to resolve. These can be dealt with in one-to-one counselling, whether by a trained counsellor, chaplain, or other member of the interdisciplinary team, but the person with AIDS must always be allowed to set his or her own time-frame for dealing with them.

PWAs find quite quickly that they have become members of a fringe group which experiences a great deal of isolation and prejudice. Margaret, a middle-aged woman who received the HIV virus through a blood transfusion, came to London and to the hospice to escape the isolation she felt within her small village. The village residents found it difficult to accept the idea that Margaret's HIV status was due to transfusion, and they assumed that it must have come from secret drug use. She felt as if they were constantly looking for needle marks on her arms and eventually Margaret felt more and more isolated within a community in which she had previously enjoyed a pleasant life. In London her daughter was able to care for her, but Margaret came to the hospice with unresolved anger about the necessary change in her mode of living. Through individual counselling she was able to come to terms with the prejudice she experienced and to share her loss.

As mentioned before, drug users carry the 'double shame' of AIDS and drugs and are perhaps the least cared for of all PWAs. It must be said that most caring agencies find drug users difficult to deal with as they bring with them their chaotic life-style. Carers are advised to take their time if possible and allow trust to develop on both sides before offering too many services. Clear boundaries, on both sides, are always advisable. Gay men have an experience of fringe group isolation and have developed what is called a 'gay life-style' in reaction to the prejudice of society at large. However, it is as well to remember that sexual activity between members of the same sex has only been decriminalised for a little over twenty years in the UK. Another aspect of isolation which produces anger among gay PWAs is the prejudice within the gay community. While many of the earliest responses to AIDS care provision came from the gay community, there is still a stigma attached to a positive HIV diagnosis. When this occurs the person with AIDS can feel profoundly isolated and rejected by those from whom he or she would normally expect acceptance. This isolation can be experienced within family groups as well, and the person with AIDS can find himself or herself an outsider within this most basic grouping. When the HIV/AIDS diagnosis is combined with a gay sexual orientation or a history of drug use, family members may well allow their prejudices to get the better of them.

Dealing with the losses brought by terminal illness is a difficult and continuing process. It is important to deal with our own death and dying issues before we can expect to be of use to PWAs. This is neglected more often than not in the training of those in the field as it is a difficult and emotionally dangerous area for all. If the counsellor has unresolved issues around death, they will surface in some form when dealing with the terminally ill, and this will confuse the therapeutic situation.

It is also important to accept the fact that not everyone will come to acceptance or even resignation and they may well die very angry and with many unresolved feelings of loss. Many who work with the terminally ill may not want to acknowledge this as they feel it reflects on the quality of hospice care. In our experience, it is the offering of care and counselling that is important rather than the results achieved. Chaplains often understand this more clearly than other members of the interdisciplinary team as they experience the impotence of helplessness on a more regular basis and do not have the structure of medical professionalism to shield them from their humanity. For this reason they can be an important resource for both PWAs and those who care for them.

A brief case history illustrates different aspects of dealing with loss. David was someone who coped by holding his feelings inside himself in an attempt to control the chaos he was feeling. He found it impossible to resign himself to his loss and wouldn't talk about his impending death, and it was obvious to his nurses that he was afraid of an emotional collapse if he did so. This was particularly difficult for some members of the team as they were looking for a 'significant' conversation during which David would share his feelings. However, David had a previous bad experience of individual counselling, and it was a slow process working towards a sense of trust with his counsellor and art therapist. He came to feel eventually that his losses were valued through drawing and painting which gave him a non-verbal channel to express his pain and to make some sense of his life. For David this was a spiritual journey, though not a traditional Christian one. The art therapist was able to give David an alternative channel for communication and expression, and the artwork became a forum in which she was able to meet him on his own terms.

The art therapist describes David's experience:

> After a hesitant start he began experimenting with the pastels. David attempted to draw the leaves on the tree outside his bedroom window, a neutral enough image one might think. However, despite efforts to draw autumn leaves he seemed only able to make them green. As David worked he began to cry. Memories of childhood and the happiness he had then suddenly sprang to mind, and the aspirations he held for himself came to the fore of his consciousness. David allowed himself to cry and to experience the grief associated with the realisation that his boyhood dreams could never come to fruition. Although initially embarrassed, he felt relieved about being able to cry. He said he did not realise that such feelings were still there within him. He made the link between the emotions that were emerging and the green leaves; green leaves that should still be on the tree but had been plucked off. David saw them representing his life coming to an end before his autumn years, plucked off the tree of life by the HIV virus. At the end of the session, David described feeling absolutely exhausted yet light inside as though a burden had been lifted.

In the next few days, David was able to discuss what he was trying to say in his art work and eventually to share his feelings with his partner who was terrified at the prospect of losing him.

One of the most complex issues surrounding AIDS is the amazing amount of guilt engendered by all concerned. Perhaps this is due to the fact that in our society the two have been so closely linked. In the early 1980s there was a good deal of talk about judgement, both from religious and secular sources, and the idea that PWAs had been irresponsible sexually was popular. All of us carry around unresolved feelings of guilt; that is part of the human condition. During times of illness these guilty feelings can be highlighted and during a terminal illness, especially one which is often linked with sexual transmission, the burden can become intolerable. Therefore, it is not surprising that guilt is one of the largest issues confronting interdisciplinary team care in hospices, and one with which all members of the team must deal. One of the most difficult aspects of guilt is that it is often not rational. One mother came to the hospice weighed down with guilt about injecting her young haemophiliac son with Factor 8 blood product which carried the HIV virus. Although she did so on the advice of her doctor, she still felt responsible for making her son HIV positive. It is not uncommon for mothers and grandmothers to feel guilty about transmitting haemophilia to their sons who in turn became infected with the HIV virus. Drug users can feel guilty about a wasted life while gay men often carry guilt concerning the pain they have caused their families due to their gay life-style. Another difficult quality unique to these deep guilty feelings is that knowing that the feelings are unjustified does not expiate them. Sexuality concerns produce almost unlimited possibilities for guilt, all the way from feeling bad about being gay or past sexual practices to guilt about passing the HIV virus on to sexual partners. Religious beliefs of all types are closely tied in with guilt as religion often uses this method for social and spiritual control. Spiritual guilt is not erased by reassurances that God loves and accepts everyone, and it is only through time spent counselling and modelling acceptance that the guilt can be reduced. Survivors usually carry some guilt about being left behind, especially if they are not HIV positive. Those caring for PWAs will find that the seeds of guilt flower easily when they fall on the fertile ground of AIDS-related illnesses.

Charles is a good illustration of the difficulties facing the interdisciplinary team when dealing with guilt issues. He was an older haemophiliac who had been terribly unlucky. In his life he had only needed Factor 8 twice, and it was on one of these occasions that the HIV virus was transmitted. He came to the hospice saying that he felt like a leper, and in fact he was admitted for respite care due to severe disfiguring dermatitis. His family could not accept his diagnosis and treated him like an outcast. He ate with his two teenage children but was asked to use different crockery and to wash up separately. His bed sheets were sent to a professional laundry, and the family avoided close contact with him. Within a few days of admission, his dermatitis cleared up, and he began one-to-one counselling sessions. During counselling Charles shared his feelings of guilt about 'infecting' himself with the virus and about leaving his family alone. He made excuses for their behaviour, and it was clear that he felt he deserved to carry these feelings. This was clearly a family problem; however, the family was unwilling to participate in family therapy and rarely visited him during his stays for respite care. A pattern developed of Charles returning home for a few weeks, only to be readmitted for dermatitis. While in the hospice, he would be taken out for walks and to the theatre, he would be treated like any other patient when it came to bathing and eating, and human contact was not avoided. After a short time his skin would clear up, and he would return home, and the pattern would be repeated. It must be said that Charles' family was not uncaring or unloving, but they were so bound up by their fears that they could not move outside their terror.

Charles came to understand this and to accept the fact that they were unable to work towards a resolution of their fears. His burden of guilt was reduced by this understanding, but the key to the release of guilt was the care and human contact he received while in the hospice. He met other men who had become HIV positive in a similar manner, and this helped him to put his guilt into perspective.

We cannot leave the issue of guilt without discussing some

suggestions concerning what assistance can be provided in a hospice setting. Perhaps the most important thing on offer is a safe place in which to look at guilt issues, especially if the patient is admitted for respite care. However, due to the nature of the AIDS-related illnesses there is never enough time to do in-depth work aimed towards resolving deep-seated guilt. It is because of the time limitations that the importance of care and acceptance is emphasised. Through contact with other patients, one-to-one counselling, and care which focuses on the needs and priorities of the patient, the PWA can find a 'safe harbour' for a time. In this supportive and understanding environment the guilty feelings often can be put into perspective. On a practical level, the interdisciplinary team can bring people together, offer family therapy, write letters for the resident, and encourage him or her to make efforts toward reconciliation. The chaplain may be the team member who can deal with spiritual guilt, but this is not always the case. Often the counsellor or nurse will act in this role with the chaplain as backup. At this time the most appropriate means of expiating spiritual guilt should be sought; this may be through rituals of the church such as confession, baptism or confirmation or through other means which might include spiritual counselling or a personal act of contrition. Again, perhaps the most important role which can be played by a hospice interdisciplinary team is that of offering a time and space to look at guilt issues in a supportive environment.

The same can be said concerning death issues, and hospice residents vary in the manner in which they come to terms with death. Some come to an acceptance of their terminal diagnosis and await death comfortably, often after a good deal of emotional and spiritual work. However, the more common scenario is a resignation to the inevitable while still fighting for control and raging to live. If the AIDS-related illnesses have been of long duration and the patient has experienced a great deal of pain and suffering, death can become a welcome relief for some. Perhaps the saddest response is by those PWAs who retreat into their fear and withdraw from human contact. They do not deny the inevitability of death, but they cannot bring themselves to talk about it. PWAs will react individually to the prospect of death and this fact, combined with some differences unique to the AIDS situation, create a challenge for those involved in AIDS hospice care. It is worth discussing some of these unique qualities.

The deathbed scene may happen several times for PWAs due to the nature of the AIDS-related illnesses. It is not uncommon for PWAs to come close to death from pneumonia several times in the course of their illness.

Ignatius was admitted to the hospice with a terminal diagnosis, and the interdisciplinary team did not expect him to live out the week. He was comatose, severely wasted, and his breathing was laboured and shallow. Some time during the first week of his stay, Ignatius had a seizure during the night and fell out of his bed. When the nurses found him he was awake and speaking in a confused manner; however, within twenty-four hours he was up in the day room talking with fellow residents. Ignatius continued to improve and eventually went home to sheltered housing. During the next three months he re-established contacts with his sister, and his parents visited from Jamaica which was made possible by his hospice counsellor who raised the air fare from charities. Eventually the deathbed scene was repeated for Ignatius and he died peacefully.

As many PWAs are young men and women, age can give a unique perspective on death. This can be very difficult for parents who naturally expect to die before their children. In our experience young people sometimes can come to terms with death more easily than the middle-aged PWA, but this is not always true. Earlier we discussed the pain of loss faced by young people when they grieve for a life that was barely lived. The sadness involved here will also affect the younger nurses who may well be caring for people near their own ages, and the interdisciplinary team as well as the family, friends, and partners may need extra bereavement care when faced with the death of a young person.

Patients also will be affected by the 'death pictures' held in their minds. PWAs may have seen lots of friends die of AIDS and may have developed terrifying images of bad deaths. The interdisciplinary team can suggest coping strategies which are designed to lessen these negative images.

These may be as simple as having someone to sit with them around the clock, being nursed in a sitting position rather than lying down, or having the lights and television on all the time. Other coping mechanisms include planning their funeral which most people want to reflect their own personalities through choice of setting, music, and readings as well as deciding how their remains will be disposed of. Perhaps two of the most useful coping strategies are the making of a last will and the provision of a 'living will'. This is a document which is a written statement of a patient's wishes regarding medical treatment at the end of life. It means that the medical staff and others around will know the patient's wishes should he or she become unable to communicate them directly. The living will also allows the PWA to name a friend or relative to take part in medical decisions on their behalf if they become incapable of doing so; this is known as a 'health care proxy'. Living wills have become common practice in the United States and recently have been introduced into the United Kingdom through a co-operative effort between the Terrence Higgins Trust and the Centre of Medical Law and Ethics at King's College, London.

The hospice setting also gives residents an opportunity to explore spiritual issues as they approach death if they wish. Most AIDS hospices have provision for this work, and many chaplains are an integral part of the interdisciplinary team. Like any other therapy or service offered in a hospice setting, the discussion of spiritual issues is offered and sometimes encouraged, but not insisted upon. As said before, the chaplain's role might well be played by some other member of the team, but the issues will be the same. The important thing to keep in mind is that the agenda must be set by the person with AIDS, not the spiritual friend or minister of religion. Another key factor in determining the success of this work is honesty on all issues. Some chaplains may need to present the views of their denomination as well as their own personal views and allow the patient to come to his or her own decision. The most common questions encountered in our experience are around the issues of judgement and afterlife, and these will be discussed in the next section of this chapter. These discussions can be facilitated by the use of family trees, artwork, biblical counselling, and rituals of particular faith traditions. It is important that if the PWA expresses a religious preference at admission the appropriate minister, rabbi, priest, or holy person is contacted in advance if possible. Dying patients may well want to reclaim the faith rituals of their childhood at the time of death, and if these are not familiar to the interdisciplinary team delay and confusion will result if preparations are not made early on.

The final unique aspect of dealing with PWAs who approach death is the request for euthanasia. When the patient has been enduring a long siege of illness it is not uncommon for a fatal injection to be requested, and this is often difficult for the staff who focus on preserving life. A helpful way of seeing this type of request is that it is a means for the person with AIDS to express anguish, pain, and frustration. When this is listened to and acknowledged the interdisciplinary team member can explain the possibilities of what can be done. It is at this time that the fears around dying can be unpacked and then addressed. Most of the big fears will be made up of small fears, and these can be dealt with, one by one. For instance, many terminal patients are afraid of choking or bleeding to death. These fears can be relieved, and as the little fears disappear the larger fear of death itself is diminished. In conclusion we want to emphasise the importance of giving the person with AIDS back as much control of his or her life as possible. It is not the job of the team to solve all the patients' problems, but to enable them to cope creatively with the last important stage of living . . . dying.

In a hospice setting it is almost inevitable that spiritual issues will be addressed at some point in time. It is quite natural to examine basic beliefs when faced with death, and this can be a creative time of growth and development. As a response to these needs, hospices have included chaplains as part of the interdisciplinary team from the founding of the modern hospice movement by Dame Cicely Saunders in South London to the growth of AIDS hospices in the 1980s. While many hospices in the UK were developed with a specifically Christian ethos they include part-time chaplains of all major faith traditions. Even the secular hospices encourage residents to ask about and to explore spiritual issues if they wish.

As with most of the therapies offered in modern hospices, the key to working with PWAs on spiritual issues is that the impetus must come from the individual rather than from the outside. On admission patients are usually asked if they have a religious preference and if they would like a visit from the appropriate chaplain. If not, it is left there until the PWA decides otherwise. Some chaplains feel that it is important to make an initial visit to all new residents even if only to introduce themselves. Many times it is at this meeting that the chaplain can explain what the hospice offers in the way of worship, study, and spiritual counselling or make arrangements to contact the appropriate religious figure, such as a rabbi, imam, or holy man. At this time it is especially important not to take advantage of the vulnerability of the person with AIDS; entering a hospice can be a difficult step for the terminally ill. Additionally, it is important to be aware that many people have a residual respect for clergy and will agree to visits just to please them.

As any member of the clergy will understand, the role of chaplain can vary greatly according to the needs of individual patients. Some will need a friend with whom to share their fears, some will need a formal representative of their faith who will bring them 'the Church' in his or her presence, and others will need someone to challenge them and with whom they can explore their relationship with God. It is also important to understand that people will bring many agendas about the church with them including a good deal of anger and pain, and these can be focused on priests and ministers. This can be especially true of male ministers who bring with them, consciously or unconsciously, a tradition of male domination and patriarchy that some may find difficult to accept.

It will be interesting to see the role of Anglican women priests develop. In the United States women priests have played a key role in the healing and pastoral ministry to PWAs bringing the sacraments and a sense of reconciliation with God into situations which their male colleagues find difficult to gain access. In the UK women deacons and religious have extended the traditional roles of nurse and counsellor to include pastor, spiritual friend, and now sacramental minister.

The need for women in this important role is clearly seen in the case of Roseanne who was one of the first female residents at the Mildmay. She was a tough young woman who had a long history of drug use during her short life. As a young girl she had been abused by her father and eventually escaped from home to live the chaotic, nomadic life of a biker. When she entered the hospice for terminal care Roseanne was angry, frightened and confused, but one of things she was sure about was that she didn't want to hear stories about a father in heaven. Roseanne's image of fatherhood was so damaged by her early childhood experience that she could not relate to traditional Christian models of God, but she did express a need for spiritual guidance and befriending. Eventually the female staff and counsellor took on the role which might have been served by the chaplain and were challenged by Roseanne to find appropriate religious symbols to express theological concepts. Although not trained in any formal sense, the women focused their discussions with Roseanne on the image of God as the Good Shepherd, and Roseanne found comfort in seeing God as caring for his lost sheep, with whom she identified. She took strength from having Psalm 23 read to her, and when she planned her funeral it was included in place of the Lord's Prayer.

Roseanne's needs and experience are interesting for two reasons; firstly because they emphasise the important role of the pastoral ministry of women working with PWAs. Many gay male clergy have been attracted to this work for a variety of positive and negative reasons, but there is an unfulfilled need for women who can bring unique gifts to the work from a sacramental perspective. In Roseanne's situation it would have been interesting and creative if a female priest had been available. Secondly, Roseanne is an example of someone for whom the patriarchal models of God were inappropriate. Women theologians are producing work in this area which would be of use to PWAs. It is not only women who cannot accept masculine religious symbolism. Many PWAs find themselves on the fringe of Christian communities, and it is a fact that gay men, drug users, and people with the HIV virus do not always fit comfortably into church congregations. Viewing Christ as friend, brother, or partner is often much more useful when attempting to reconcile one's life with God. In Roseanne's case it was the counsellor and female staff members who could relate to her anger and pain around men because of their own experience as women. They had not necessarily been abused as children, but as women they were able to understand Roseanne's pain and thereby assist with the healing process.

Regardless of who is chosen to work on spiritual issues, the important question to be answered is, 'What do PWAs who enter a hospice look for when it comes to spiritual guidance?' Father Bernard Lynch, radical Roman Catholic priest, who has devoted over ten years of his life to working in AIDS both in the US and here, says there are two basic questions asked by PWAs: 'Who is God?' and 'What about afterlife?' We do not find this surprising as these are the same questions asked by all people of faith throughout the ages, but they take on an immediacy in terminal care which is lacking in day-to-day life. Some traditions will offer concrete answers to these complex questions, and for some this will be adequate; however, others will require more searching and exploration of spiritual issues, and they may well not come to any conclusion as they approach death. In this situation the search and the journey are as important as the conclusion, and the chaplain in an AIDS hospice must honour this approach regardless of his or her own specific beliefs.

As with other aspects of care and counselling of PWAs, spirituality presents unique challenges and opportunities. Some of these include working interdenominationally, the integration of ritual and sacramental ministry into pastoral care, and unique coping strategies, such as bargaining. Most AIDS hospices will have representatives of all faith traditions as part of the care services offered. In a Christian hospice the chaplain will be a key worker on the interdisciplinary team and will give important input in making decisions about care plans and counselling provision. The chaplain will also have the opportunity of developing an ecumenical team of chaplains to work with PWAs from a wide variety of faith backgrounds, such as the one developed by Peter Clarke at Mildmay AIDS Hospice. Here part-time volunteer chaplains from Roman Catholic, Anglican, Baptist, and Methodist traditions meet monthly to discuss individual residents and to support one another. At the same time the full-time chaplains will liaise with Hindu, Muslim, and Jewish colleagues when appropriate. Since most clergy tend to remain within tight denominational boundaries, this working model gives them an opportunity to observe and to share with others in a useful and practical manner. Where more than one chaplain has worked with a resident it is quite common for the funeral to be shared. When Scottie, a devout high-church Anglican from a Roman Catholic background, died his parish priest took the funeral. As mentioned in a previous chapter, Scottie had been a long term resident in the hospice and came to know several of the chaplains. When it was time for the funeral, the parish priest was assisted at the altar by the volunteer Anglican chaplain and the hospice chaplain who was a Baptist.

The importance of ritual and sacramental ministry cannot be underestimated in hospice work. As residents approach the end of their lives, it is not uncommon for them to revert to the tradition of their childhood religious backgrounds. They have a vestigial memory of the use of ritual and the sustaining, supportive role it can play and may well ask for confession, baptism, or confirmation.

Freddie came to the hospice for respite care and developed a relationship with his counsellor which included discussions about spiritual issues. He lived in South London and when he was well enough would walk along the Embankment to Southwark Cathedral where he would sit quietly. At the time of his visits Southwark was preparing the St Andrew's Chapel for dedication to PWAs, and Freddie would sit and watch the work. While resident in the hospice he asked to see the Anglican chaplain and talked with him about his childhood experiences in the Church of England. Freddie had been a choirboy in the 1950s and wanted very much to be confirmed with his classmates at fourteen. However, he felt it wouldn't be allowed since he knew he was gay and he eventually left the church. Through discussion with the chaplain it became clear that Freddie wanted to reclaim his faith and was assured that his sexuality would be no bar to confirmation. At the same time, Freddie wanted his family to accept him before he died, and the chaplain suggested that he be confirmed in a private family service at the cathedral. Having the approval of his church through the ritual of confirmation in the presence of his family, partner, and friends was the outward sign of God's love and acceptance for Freddie. On a Sunday afternoon in the spring before he died, Freddie was confirmed at Southwark Cathedral just as he had wanted. The Bishop visited him in his home prior to the service and the chapel was filled with those who loved and cared for him.

More commonplace use of sacramental ministry is important as well. If the person with AIDS is accustomed to receiving communion on a weekly basis and/or attending services, it is important that this pattern should continue. Religious observance is one of the few activities which can provide continuity throughout a long period of illness, and also one which is deeply rooted in a person's identity. In our experience spiritual work in a hospice setting may well focus on images of God and afterlife as Father Lynch says, but it often will include a need for reconciliation whether through prayer, discussion or formal ritual. Many PWAs will be carrying a burden of guilt about past behaviour or relationships and will need a means of releasing that pain. Formal confession can do this as can the laying on of hands in the context of prayer or the giving of a simple blessing. In the Anglican and Roman Catholic traditions, the use of holy oils blessed by the bishop on Maundy Thursday will carry special significance for those desiring healing. When the oils are used as part of a blessing or anointing of the sick the presence of God is symbolised for the person with AIDS. The ritual is allowed to take the place of words which often protect us from our feelings, and we are able to experience God in a deep non-verbal way.

One of the unique spiritual issues which surfaces throughout the pastoral care of PWAs is the need to confront guilt. One of the commonest means for patients is bargaining. This is a difficult situation for most people of faith as they do not see God as a something to be placated through promises of good behaviour. This becomes especially complex when dealing with the terminally ill. In our experience, drug users often use bargaining as a means of giving up drugs, sometimes even going as far as stopping their methadone. The unstated bargain is that if they stop drugs then God won't allow them to die just yet. It takes a sensitive pastor to confront this type of thinking and to move the person with AIDS gently towards an understanding of a concept of God who meets us where we are at the moment without requiring any special conditions.

Other means of coping by bargaining include a reversion to a childish relationship with God. Often this is modelled on the image of God retained from early years and presents difficulty for the chaplain because of the disparity between the mature adult and the immature theological point of view. The challenge for the chaplain is to allow the person the comfort of the surety of the past while encouraging spiritual growth. Another manifestation of this type of bargaining is the last minute request for a minister or rabbi from an ostensibly non-practising patient. Sometimes this request is encouraged by family members who look towards a 'religious expert' who will know about last things and the afterlife. The positive side of this development is the growing number of requests for prayers and communion around the bedside of the dying. Families, friends, and partners are finding comfort in the sense of bonding which comes from this practice.

At the beginning of this chapter we spoke about the unique aspects of working with PWAs. Counselling and pastoral care work in the field draws on traditional techniques, but it is the situation in which they are used which presents the challenge. Some of the creative responses used in the work have been discussed with an emphasis on the interdisciplinary approach. In conclusion, the element which needs to be emphasised again and again is that the hospice approach derives from the needs and desires of the patient. For as long as possible, the person with AIDS will be the key figure in determining his or her care plan, particularly when it comes to counselling and pastoral care.

5

BEREAVEMENT

There is a great deal of very good material published about bereavement, and it is not our intention to repeat what had been said by others. However, there are specific areas when dealing with HIV/AIDS which need special attention. It is the issues surrounding homophobia, survivor guilt, prejudice, multiple bereavement, good and bad death experiences, support for families and partners, and the role of memorial services in the grieving process on which we will focus our discussion.

When dealing with anyone experiencing a loss it is important to remember that bereavement is not a sickness; it is a natural process which every human being experiences at some time in life. Too frequently intervention by well-meaning counsellors, and others, removes natural coping mechanisms. Only when there are other issues or concurrent life crises does the professional need to be around. This is true with AIDS, and if it is compounded by old grief and problems, secrets, experiences of homophobia and prejudice this will affect the bereavement process.

We have some concern about what is becoming a 'bereavement industry' which is filled with courses, books, workshops, and training programmes, and we are fearful that counselling is becoming a subsidiary of that industry. One of the most disturbing aspects of this trend is that some of the training courses are very short, some only over a weekend, and it is possible that these bereavement workers may step beyond the boundaries of their brief training. Most people won't need professional help with their bereavement and only need the support of family and friends. People suffering a loss should be warned about being caught up in the bereavement industry and be encouraged to grieve for the person they have lost using the natural forms of support which surround them. If there are other factors which impair the grieving process then help from a professional counsellor or pastor can be sought.

There is no doubt that homophobia is an important element in the grieving process for most people who have a gay family member or partner dying from HIV/AIDS. It is also an unacknowledged element within the family dynamic as sexuality is not often talked about in family groups. Not all the family may know that the person dying is gay, and some won't be able to acknowledge the fact if told. Having a gay son is often a family secret which is guarded closely by the female family members and not acknowledged by the male members. This is made more difficult when someone is dying of AIDS; the family will find it difficult to deny a gay member's homosexuality. A counsellor in the hospice says, 'I don't know how many times a mother or sister has taken me aside and said, "I know, and you know, what the truth is, but we're not going to talk about it." In the States this would be approached quite differently and the family member might well say, "I know, and you know, and we MUST talk about it." It should be asked if this is healthier?'

Families will find themselves challenged to confront their own homophobia, and they will often experience guilt about their feelings. Anger at the child who died of AIDS is also a common feeling as is anger at the gay life-style. 'If my son hadn't been gay he wouldn't have died', is a common lament by parents. These feelings will confuse and complicate the grieving process. The family may keep secret the cause of death and then grief becomes filtered in order to protect the AIDS diagnosis becoming known. This is also true of parents of drug users as they can experience the double shame of AIDS and drugs. The grieving process is then impaired due to this secrecy, and it is appropriate for the hospice to offer family therapy. Families and partners grieving for a loved one who has died of AIDS will usually experience less support from society at large because of prejudice about PWAs. This may be particularly painful for homophobic parents and family members as they suddenly find the tables turned on them as they experience some of the prejudice they previously projected on to PWAs or gay people. Often the anger of homophobic families can be focused on the surviving partner of their gay son, and this confuses the partner's grieving. Their position in the family constellation is not clear, and they are usually denied the position of chief mourner. At the same time if the partner is not open about his homosexuality at work, he will not be offered compassionate leave, and society will deny him the right to mourn his loss while the family takes charge of grieving.

Homophobic families can impose their anger and guilt on the bereavement process and create an atmosphere of distrust and secrecy. This can take the form of demanding separate funeral services for their son, assigning the partner and friends to a memorial service while they then take the body back to the home town for burial. It is not uncommon for families to demand that the minister say nothing about the cause of death and not to mention the name of the hospice where their son died in case someone were to associate the hospice and AIDS. If their son's partner and friends are allowed to attend the funeral, they invariably occupy separate sides of the chapel. On the other hand, it is possible for the family to be shut out by a close-knit circle of gay friends who make up an alternative extended family. A skilled and compassionate chaplain might be able to effect some healing through a sensitive service which emphasises the things which the two groups share in common, namely the life of the person they loved. If possible a service which combines aspects of the PWAs life, the family, gay friends, and work colleagues is the most appropriate vehicle for accomplishing this.

Paul's partner, Tim, died in the hospice and his funeral service was planned by Paul and his partner's mother. Although the couple were not religious, Tim's family were devout Anglicans and one of the brothers was an Anglican priest, so care was taken to design a service which would honour both sides of Tim's life. Tim's brother was never able to accept his sexuality and refused to visit Tim when he fell ill and prevented his wife and children from doing so. Unfortunately, it was only after Tim's death that the brother began to ameliorate his views. The hospice counsellor was able to meet with Paul and Tim's mother to plan a service which would represent both sides of Tim's life. At the funeral Tim's mother sat with Paul as co-chief mourners, and Paul gave a short talk about his partner. Each side gave a little and some reconciliation was effected. Tim's mother was particularly pleased when the brother attended the funeral with his own family.

Guilt is a common feeling among those experiencing a bereavement, but in HIV/AIDS prolonged survivor guilt is often a problem. This usually takes the form of idealisation of the lost partner or family member with a consequent need to punish themselves. This is a means of distancing oneself from the feelings of loss, and it is the task of the counsellor or pastor to assist the survivor in moving on in his or her bereavement by examining the relationship honestly and openly. Survivor guilt appears in all groups experiencing loss through HIV/AIDS but can be particularly complicated with gay men. They may well have suffered several losses from AIDS, and it is common that the grieving process for one person is hardly begun before another dies. Graeme, who came to the hospice chaplain for counselling said:

> I no longer go to funerals; when I reached ten I stopped. I began to wonder what I was doing to myself; I had no place for the pain and anger to go before it was time to put on 'the suit' and go off to another funeral. If I gave each friend I've lost a year of grief I'd be fifty before I caught up with those who've died as of now. I'm constantly depressed and I have to find some way out of this.

Graeme was on the verge of shutting off his feelings in an attempt to protect himself from overwhelming grief and fear. The situation was complicated further by the fact that Graeme was HIV positive. For gay men the additional uncertainty about their own health status is often a hidden but powerful complication. It is important for the counsellor or pastor to recognise the function of the depression and guilt which is used to avoid other feelings. In most cases these will include fear and anxiety about what lies ahead for them. The task is to avoid falling into the litany of 'I should have . . . I could have . . . I didn't bother . . . I'm responsible . . .' and to work sensitively in exploring the avoided feelings.

Multiple bereavements are becoming more and more common in HIV/AIDS as it moves into the heterosexual family and the drug using population. At the hospice at Mildmay we are seeing more and more African families who have both HIV positive and dying members. It is not uncommon for a nuclear family to have lost members of their extended family both here and back in Africa. While part of a hospice teaching team in Africa one of us visited the mother of a woman who died of AIDS at the Mildmay. During the visit the mother revealed that two of her other children had died of AIDS and that she was taking care of the three remaining grandchildren. It is a common sight in Africa to see old grandparents raising very young children.

Another family at the hospice presented a similar sad story. Regina is a young African woman with a small child; her husband has already died of AIDS. Her brother and a sister have also died and one sister remains. As Regina works to deal with the many bereavements in her life, she is faced with her own deteriorating health and the problem facing her about the care and custody of her own daughter in the future. Clearly these are examples of extended and complicated bereavement and would take many hours of skilled loss counselling merely to begin to overcome. However, when the survivor is facing HIV/AIDS-related illnesses themselves that time often is not there. Some of the helpful methods suggested by bereavement experts are the use of life stories, trees of life, and loss histories. These exercises can help break protective patterns in grief and assist the survivor in experiencing his or her feelings.

The experience of funerals can have a profound effect on the grieving process. This is particularly true with HIV/AIDS since the practice of undertakers and crematoria staff is not always sensitive. Good funerals are an important part of the healing process. The trend in the US toward memorial services where the body is not present which replace traditional services in church or at the crematorium is to be deplored. This can contribute to a denial of loss and severely impede the grieving process in our opinion. The importance of ritual which acts as a vehicle to carry and to express the pain of loss cannot be overemphasised. A good funeral will give the mourners an opportunity to express and to release their pain in a form to which they can relate. The cultural norms of the mourners provide a socially acceptable form of grieving and comfort regardless of their cultural or faith backgrounds.

We can say without hesitation that funerals planned by those who have died are without exception 'good funerals'. In this circumstance the mourners are made to feel like guests at a final farewell, and the funeral expresses a picture of the full person. This would describe all well-planned funerals and this picture would include family, friends, partners, and work colleagues as well as the deceased's personality expressed through readings, music, and the form of service.

This was certainly true of Gary's funeral which he had planned with care well before his final illness. Although the service was performed within the context of Christian traditions, it was a uniquely personal experience. Gary was a keen opera enthusiast and it seemed particularly appropriate when his coffin made its exit at the crematorium completely covered in white lilies, orchids, and stephanotis to Wagner's 'Ride of the Valkyries'. This dramatic ending expressed Gary's love of the theatrical and personal drama which had been such an important part of his life. The hospice chaplain who took Gary's funeral said:

> Gary asked me to sprinkle his coffin with holy water before the music began, so I was busy with that when the Wagner began. I looked out at the congregation as the coffin moved away and was confronted with a crowd of smiles. There were some tears, but I'd say they were very healthy tears . . . more like tears of goodbye and regret at a sad parting. Later Gary's mother said to me, 'Thank you for the funeral; it was so *Gary*.'

Funerals like Gary's play an important role in the grieving process, but unfortunately this is not always the case. Bad practice does occur, but we feel that this is much less common than in the past. Through lobbying from AIDS hospices and caring agencies there is a much more welcoming attitude on the part of undertakers, and it is fair to say that AIDS hospices have helped to set the standard for good practice in AIDS funerals. By adopting good practice themselves and refusing to recommend clergy, crematoria, or undertakers who were not sensitive to the special needs of those experiencing a loss from AIDS, the standards were soon set. It is standard practice in most health care settings to place the body of a person with AIDS in a zipped plastic body bag. Few hospices use body bags any longer, but mourners sometimes find undertakers hesitant about letting them view the body once it has left the hospice. It is important that enough time is allowed for visits by family, friends, and partners, so that they are left with a realistic and positive last image. Mourners who view the body of a loved one may take away a negative image if the body is not presented in a sensitive manner and setting. Making sure the death certificate doesn't state AIDS as cause of death is standard practice today; this prevents any possible prejudice when the mourners make the preparations for the funeral, register the death, and deal with the deceased's personal business.

Two other considerations are important during initial bereavement which if ignored can result in a negative experience. Firstly, the chaplain or counsellor who is working with the mourners to arrange the funeral service must be careful not to superimpose a false set of religious values on the survivors. It is important to take time to listen to what is really being said by the family and friends as well as enquiring sensitively about the person's religious beliefs. Death from AIDS-related illnesses is experienced by people of all religious faiths and from a variety of cultures. If counsellors and pastors are to be useful to this pluralistic community, they will need to have some understanding of the major world faiths and their mourning traditions. People who espouse no faith at all may want a non-religious funeral which can be just as effective a ritual form of farewell. The second consideration is that PWAs may well have competing sets of mourners with competing sets of religious and spiritual values. In this case it is of paramount importance to find out what the PWA believed and might have wanted. When that is done it is possible to begin to suggest alternatives and to negotiate a funeral and mourning process which could meet varying sets of needs.

If the bereavement process is impaired by homophobia, multiple bereavement, previous bad experiences with funerals or other factors, bereavement support is offered by most hospices. In AIDS hospices this can take the form of one-to-one counselling with a counsellor or pastor, a partners' support group, or family counselling. However, it must be said that we do not automatically recommend bereavement counselling for everyone experiencing loss, and we emphasise again that bereavement is a natural process which is often best handled by family and friends. We do make referrals to other excellent bereavement counselling organisations such as Cruse, Compassionate Friends, and the National Association of Bereavement Services for family members living outside the hospice's local area. As in all counselling situations it is important to establish the boundaries when entering into a contract for a specific number of one-to-one or group counselling sessions. Clear boundaries in bereavement counselling assist the mourner in establishing trust and an environment in which he or she may explore and experience his or her fears and feelings. In hospice bereavement counselling we are seeing more children than ever before, and they often present unusual challenges. Terry asked the hospice counsellor if he could come to her as he needed to ask some questions that he couldn't ask his parents. As a twelve-year-old this was his first experience of death; he knew his brother who died was gay and that he died of AIDS. Terry also knew his other brother was gay, and his grief was intensified by his uncertainty about his own sexual identity. Initially he wanted information about HIV transmission and about gay sex. Later questions about his own sexuality emerged, and he wondered if he was destined to be gay also. These were issues which were most appropriately dealt with in one-to-one counselling, and once they were discussed Terry could begin his grieving for his brother. Children do grieve, even though most parents attempt to shield them from the process. Children need the opportunity to face loss as do adults and to be allowed to grieve for someone they have loved. Children of gay men who learn of their father's sexuality as teenagers appear to experience more difficulty with the grieving process. They will have a good deal to sort out about their parents' relationship, and it is especially difficult for children in their early teens who are just beginning to be aware of their sexuality.

Family therapy is an important means of coming to terms with loss as it gives the family group an opportunity to talk around the grief process and how it has affected the family dynamic. Usually this work is offered only to locally based families, but some will travel a good distance to family therapy sessions at the hospice where their PWA has died. Some of the important issues likely to emerge include parents blaming one another for their child's sexuality or drug use, acceptance of homosexuality by siblings, access to family secrets and the anger surrounding why some are allowed to know and others not, and feelings about the surviving partner. It is in these family situations that anger is expressed at the deceased by contesting the will or rejecting a partner.

Partners are offered the option of joining a partners' bereavement group, and in our experience most take up the offer. In the beginning these groups were entirely composed of gay men, but as the HIV/AIDS scene has changed so has the composition of the groups. At the Mildmay the groups are open to any survivor of a Mildmay patient. Following the death a letter is sent to everyone involved with the PWA inviting them to participate in a group of eight people for six months. The group is facilitated by a counsellor, but there is a group life and identity. The group has a closed membership in order for trust to develop, and attendance and confidentiality are also key factors in developing trust. Subjects will vary according to the needs and experiences of group members, but all begin by sharing their experiences of the Mildmay. Other areas covered might include secrets about sexuality, the need to have their grief valued, funeral experiences, anger, loneliness, the need to replace the lost one, guilt, support networks, and the reality and fantasies about their own health status. Group members move at their own pace, and a good deal of time is spent looking at the past and present. All members have lost partners at approximately the same time, so they are experiencing similar feelings of grief and loss. As the group approaches its sixth month, time is spent examining the pain of endings. This will be another loss for them, and in some sense the ending of the group becomes a mirror of how they are dealing with their own personal loss. The six-month limit is kept to closely, as dependency is always a danger in bereavement work. Some group members continue to meet socially, and this is encouraged as the basis is changed from bereavement work to socialising and support.

We conclude this chapter with a discussion of the role of memorial services in the grieving process for survivors of PWAs. Here we are speaking about a corporate expression of grief in a supportive context, namely the hospice. Most hospices organise memorial services several times a year to remember those who died. In an AIDS hospice such as the Mildmay, the service is designed to give value to an individual's grief in that the interdisciplinary team organise and put on the service for the survivors. On the evening of the service there is no need for secrets as all those attending have lost people they have loved to AIDS. This is especially important for families and partners who have not been able to discuss publicly the cause of death. The memorial service can be reconciling by bringing together disparate groups in a less threatening and stressful situation than the funeral. As the memorial service will be weeks or months after the death, people are able to relate more easily and comfortably. As mentioned earlier in this chapter, Tim's brother began to face his anger and guilt when he attended the funeral with his family. Three months later he came to the memorial service, again with his family, and began tentative steps toward accepting Paul as chief mourner for his brother.

The form of service at the Mildmay is a good example of a sensitive and effective co-operation between chaplaincy and counselling areas, but the entire hospice staff lead the service. This may include housekeepers reading a lesson, a volunteer chaplain preaching, or family members lighting the candle of remembrance. The services are held three times a year, and anyone who was known to be important to the person with AIDS is invited and 85 per cent of these accept the invitation, some coming from long distances and foreign countries. Professionals who were involved in the care of the PWA outside of the hospice are invited as well. A central part of the service is given over to the reading of the first names of all those who have died in the hospice in the last four months which is preceded by the lighting of a candle by a partner, parent, or family member to symbolise all those being remembered. This simple act effectively unites all those attending in a collective expression of grief. An important part of the evening is the opportunity for all those attending to speak with interdisciplinary team staff members if they wish. During refreshments following the service those attending can see the name of their person with AIDS written in the Book of Remembrance which is normally on display in the chapel and meet team staff. The memorial service is also an opportunity for the busy HIV/AIDS care professionals to acknowledge their grief. In addition to the regular memorial services each person involved with a PWA who died at the Mildmay receives a remembrance card on the first anniversary of the death.

We have emphasised in this chapter that bereavement is a natural process. However, the counsellor and pastor can facilitate the process when there are complicating factors. Even so, the real work must be done by the individual, and we are impressed by the courage to continue to live in the face of many complicating factors shown by the survivors with whom we have worked.

6

PRACTICAL CONCERNS

In the past few years, new issues have come up for the caring community working with PWAs, and many of these issues don't fall within the traditional areas covered by counsellors. However, in a hospice situation with an interdisciplinary team working model these community-based concerns are addressed. A growing number of PWAs have immigration and visa problems, and these problems are now extending into the families as we are seeing more and more patients from Africa. This chapter will discuss these issues as well as the quite practical problems surrounding arranging funerals, welfare, housing, registering deaths, and after-death care for surviving partners and family members.

Practical concerns are becoming more important because people are living longer with an AIDS diagnosis. The issues surrounding housing, welfare benefits, home care, out-patient treatment, and daycare centres have come to the fore, and the AIDS caring community will need to use a combination of statutory and voluntary agencies to provide care for PWAs. The voluntary sector is an important part of the care picture as they are able to respond without a lot of red tape, and many of the better known groups have been doing just this for the last several years, i.e. AIDS Caring Education and Training (ACET), Terrence Higgins Trust (THT), London Lighthouse, Mildmay AIDS Hospice, the Salvation Army, and Care and Resources for People Affected by AIDS (CARA), among others. There has been a growing development of AIDS community care teams from the statutory agencies such as the pioneering Kensington and Chelsea Health Care Team, Dr Rob George's Bloomsbury Community Care Team, and St Mary's Hospital Home Support

Team, to name just a few. These groups provide home support for PWAs with a wide range of services when the patient is discharged from his or her acute-care centre or hospice. There also has been a growth in the development of housing projects aimed at HIV and AIDS residents providing low, medium, and high support levels. La Verna House in West London, and the East London Lodge Projects provide much needed sheltered housing for PWAs, and this pattern is being followed throughout the country. These developments are heartening, but it is often the hospice interdisciplinary team which deals with the final practical concerns.

Immigration and visas

It is surprising how many PWAs arrive at the hospice with these types of concerns. It would be natural to assume that immigration and visa problems would have been sorted out long before the terminal stage. However, many hospice residents enter for respite care, and some have on-going, and seemingly insoluble, immigration disputes. Of course, important work is done by the Association for Welfare of Immigrants, but the hospices are seeing a steady stream of African patients who need assistance with Home Office concerns. Some may have overstayed a holiday visa and be afraid of deportation and others may be in the process of applying for refugee status. If a PWA is facing a terminal diagnosis, it is not difficult to get a year stay extension, but if they want a family member or friend to come to be with them during their illness it can be a complicated, if not impossible, process. Our experience has been that immigration authorities often let people stay if they have HIV status, and if they have an AIDS diagnosis we have never seen them refused. Initially, these hospice residents would have very little access to the benefit system here in England other than basic income support until residency is established. Housing is often a problem if they are well enough to leave the hospice, and they can tie up a much needed hospital or hospice bed longer than they actually need it while housing is arranged. Currently, the interdisciplinary team at Mildmay AIDS Hospice is doing more work with international social services due to the fact that there are more families with children, both here and in Africa, being treated by AIDS care units. An important aspect of the changing scene in HIV/AIDS is the prospect of long-term care for children, and caring agencies here are just beginning to take this on board. Questions about what is the best alternative for children whose parents have died of AIDS will have to be considered, and most importantly, whether it is better for the children to be fostered, adopted here, or reunited with an extended family in Africa if possible.

This is the case with Agatha who has twin six-year-old boys and has been in and out of hospice care for almost a year. At the beginning of her care, the interdisciplinary team spent a good deal of time sorting out her visa problems and determining the residency status of the two boys. Since Agatha has a sister living here it made the situation a bit easier, but that has not solved the care concerns for the twins. At one point Agatha's sister was caring for the boys while Agatha was in the hospice for respite care. After some time she found it impossible to do so any longer and keep her own family life organised, so the sister turned up at the hospice one morning and left the boys at the reception desk. A long day was spent trying to sort out more support for the sister, and in the end the two boys went back to her. However, the future is extremely uncertain as it is clear they will not be fostered or adopted by her. The boys speak good English and are beginning to see the UK as their home country, and if Agatha should decide to send them back to Africa the move should be made soon. Agatha also feels pressed to make a decision about the boys before she falls ill again, and it is the uncertainty about AIDS-related illnesses which complicates the situation. While she is well currently, Agatha could contract a life threatening illness without much advance warning. The hospice counsellor and welfare officer are working with the mother to make this difficult decision.

Funerals

The interdisciplinary team finds that people often need help with the funeral arrangements because this is the first funeral they have had to face. In the case of young people dying of

AIDS, the parents are often so distressed at the prospect of arranging a funeral for one of their own children that they are disabled. It is also the case many times at the London AIDS hospices that the survivors, especially parents, are not London-based, so they are unfamiliar with undertakers, registering the death, or simply are intimidated at the idea of finding their own way around London.

Another practical concern is the death certificate. Many people have a fear as to what it will say regarding the cause of death. The handing over of this is often a multidisciplinary exercise in counselling between the nurses on the hospice ward and the hospice counsellor. Mildmay AIDS Hospice has an arrangement with the local registrar that the death certificate will give the illness that the patient actually died of, i.e. pneumonia, TB, etc., and not AIDS. The hospice then sends the registrar a covering letter for the official records. Most survivors are relieved that they will not have to take a certificate to the bank or an employer bearing the perceived stigma of AIDS. The interdisciplinary team can usually arrange for a volunteer to accompany the person registering the death, and this, combined with a careful explanation of what questions will be asked at the registrar's office, helps to alleviate anxiety. During this time the counsellor will begin to talk about the funeral and the procedures to follow in making arrangements. The staff member offers to put the partner or family in touch with the appropriate minister of religion, or offers one of the hospice chaplains to arrange the service, or guides them to organisations which will arrange a non-religious funeral such as the Humanist Association or the National Secular Society, both of whom have London offices.

Many survivors also appreciate a volunteer or counsellor to accompany them to an undertaker who will handle the arrangements sensitively, especially if they are not familiar with the area.

In chapter 2 we discussed the story of Stephen, the Canadian solicitor who chose to remain in England for treatment until he died in a hospice. He was very hesitant to have his mother visit, but at the last minute he decided the time was right. However, Stephen had left it too late, and while his mother was flying in from Victoria he died. Knowing this, the primary nurse rang the Anglican chaplain, suggesting that as he too was Canadian he might meet the mother at the airport and explain what had occurred. The chaplain agreed to go out to Gatwick and was able to spend some time in the airport's chapel with her before they came into London. It was her first trip to Europe and this, combined with her son's death only hours before, confused and disoriented the woman greatly. For the next few days she became almost totally dependent on the chaplain and asked him to accompany her through the maze of British bureaucracy which was unfamiliar to her. The chaplain took her to register the death and to make the funeral arrangements. Stephen's family was quite wealthy, but there seemed no need for an elaborate funeral since no one was expected to attend. Stephen had told no one he was ill and had refused visits from those who had learned of his condition. The chaplain encouraged the mother to choose the type of funeral she thought appropriate, and she decided on a simple coffin and service at the local crematorium. Stephen's ashes were then to be shipped home for interment in Canada by their family minister. It is quite common for bereaved parents and partners to rely heavily on hospice staff during times of unexpected death, and it was appropriate to offer Stephen's mother this much support. Not every case would demand so much individual and personal handling, but the interdisciplinary team are careful to adapt to individual needs.

It is possible to arrange a completely do-it-yourself funeral which means that all the arrangements are made by the survivors. In this case, the coffin is purchased from a supplier and transport is arranged privately. Also arrangements can be made privately with the crematorium and local clergy or others to lead the service; however, most people would prefer to leave these things to a trained and sensitive professional.

During the first few days following a death, people often do not assimilate information very quickly, and it is important that all the arrangements are also given in written form. This information includes maps to the registrar's office, the steps to follow in making funeral arrangements, and an estimate of varying costs. Most people leave money in their estate to cover a funeral, but a DSS funeral can be arranged if there is none. In this case it is the person organising the funeral who must be on benefit rather than the deceased. PWAs with no funds, next of kin, or someone able and prepared to pay for a funeral will have their funerals paid for by the local authority in which they died. Usually this provision is under contract with a specific undertaker to provide a simple funeral at the firm's convenience, but there is an option for either a burial in a plot with up to eight others or cremation.

Although people might assume there would be problems about transporting the bodies of PWAs overseas for burial or cremation, there has been no problem in our experience. The paperwork involved can be complicated, but if the family is willing to follow the procedures the body can be flown almost anywhere in the world. There is no problem whatsoever about transporting ashes for scattering or burial; it is a simple matter of sending them through the post. In all cases, the family and partners of PWAs find it a great relief if the deceased has left some idea of how he or she would like their funeral conducted. As mentioned elsewhere in this book, some PWAs will leave detailed directions about their funerals, and this is much appreciated by the survivors.

Welfare and Housing

The maze of welfare benefits available to PWAs is often confusing and often changes from one government budget to the next. When entering the hospice, many PWAs arrive with a tangle of welfare concerns, and it is the responsibility of the welfare officer to assist in sorting them out. This contributes to the well-being of the patient as it relieves an important concern, one which is quite difficult to deal with when ill. As the benefit provision is constantly changing, the welfare officer will have current knowledge as to what is available and when to apply for it. There are funds which only become available when the person with AIDS has a terminal diagnosis, and the application for these must be presented to the patient sensitively and carefully. AIDS hospices also assist with applications for similar support provision for those caring for PWAs.

The welfare officer will also know the funding sources for special needs grants to cover such things as heating, holidays, and last wishes. The last wishes often take the form of wanting a visit by an overseas relative and that can be arranged with funds from a variety of sources, mostly from voluntary agencies.

Schabel came from the Middle East about ten years ago to live and work in London. Since that time he had not returned nor had his parents been able to visit, and it was Schabel's final wish that he see them before he died. Initially, the hospice interdisciplinary team thought he might be well enough to make the trip himself if funding could be found. Working with the doctors and nursing staff, the welfare officer and counsellor canvassed the AIDS caring agencies for assistance and eventually the money for the flight was organised. However, by the time this was accomplished, Schabel's condition had deteriorated and he was in no condition for foreign travel. The team discussed the situation and decided to find the money to fly both his parents to London, but this took another week or so. When all the arrangements had been made Schabel announced that he had not told his family that he was ill and that they did not know he was gay. This new complication involved the counselling staff in some last minute negotiations with Schabel to determine how much and what he wanted to tell his parents. Schabel's sister was called in to help with the decision, and in the end she took on the job of telling the parents about their son's illness. The story does have a happy ending as Schabel's parents did come and stay at the hospice for a fortnight. It was a time of reconciliation and deepening family ties, and the interdisciplinary team felt that the amount of time they had spent making it happen had been worth the outcome. Mildmay AIDS Hospice provides a three-bedroom apartment for visits by family and friends coming from outside the area plus sleep-over facilities within the person's room.

For many people the social needs can outweigh the health considerations, and sometimes the two are inextricably combined as in the case of housing. If the PWA is in poor housing and can't meet the financial demands made upon them, their health status is both compromised and often ignored. Existing housing may need modification in order for the PWA to live there more conveniently by adding chair lifts, bath aids, rails, or an intercom. Some PWAs will need moving from an upper floor flat to the ground floor where access is easier and a wheelchair can be used if necessary. Determining the correct time to enter sheltered housing is a matter which will take careful handling as it indicates to the PWA that they are giving up important control over their life. Sometimes this decision is overtaken by the PWA's health status when it becomes obvious to all that they can no longer cope alone. As mentioned earlier sheltered housing projects for PWAs which offer a variety of care levels are being developed throughout the country. Many of these are Christian sponsored or based, and in our opinion it is a particularly appropriate area for the churches to develop.

A good example of this is the development of a redundant vicarage in East London by Sebastian Sandys. When the parish was combined with another, the team vicar continued to live in the Victorian vicarage until a new one was built. There was a plan for a private developer to convert the house to luxury flats, but in the end this fell through. It was at this time that Sebastian formulated the idea of providing housing for PWAs and began searching for funding from trusts. As in most of these cases, the work was the dream and vision of one person, assisted by a few others. The search for funding was a slow process and the group was determined to surmount the problems facing them. Eventually the property was refurbished and opened as St Barnabas House offering sheltered twenty-four hour care for six PWAs.

Wills

AIDS hospices encourage people to make wills and provide a free service to do so with volunteer solicitors attending. A similar service is available through the Terrence Higgins Trust. A will is important for many reasons including the disposal of property, pension rights, and to make sure the estate goes where the deceased intends it to go. In the case of gay relationships the partners have no legal rights unless the wishes of the deceased are clearly stated in the will. It is for this reason that it is particularly important for gay men to make wills. Pension rights, insurance payments, and voluntary pension scheme benefits can sometimes be designated to a chosen person other than the next of kin, and it is important to explore these options early on.

Benjamin and his partner, Rolf, fell into the trap of never expecting anything life threatening to come their way. When Rolf became ill with PCP and died quickly without leaving a will, Benjamin was left to sort out his estate and to make some sense out of their tangled financial arrangements. The two men had lived together for fifteen years, shared expenses, and bought a flat together. Both were civil servants and there was considerable property held in common. As in many cases, Rolf's family knew he was gay but chose not to talk about it and certainly would not acknowledge Benjamin as the chief mourner or partner with rights to share property. Following the funeral, the family made enquiries about insurance policies, ownership of the flat, Rolf's bank account, and pension contributions. Benjamin assumed all these were his since that is what he and Rolf intended. However, he soon found himself in the position of having to find a solicitor to help him protect his home and his future. Rolf had nominated Benjamin on his life insurance so that went directly to him without question, but since Rolf's bank account and building society savings account were not joint accounts, the considerable sums in these went into his estate. The provision of the pension fund was that a lump sum went to the next of kin, and again, since Rolf had not nominated Benjamin, the money went into his estate. The family also requested that Rolf's share of the flat go into the estate as well, but since the mortgage was of a type which pays itself off in full in the event of one of the parties dying, the flat came to Benjamin directly. The family then demanded sale of half the contents of the flat, and the money earned to be put into the estate.

Within weeks of losing his partner of fifteen years, Benjamin was facing the prospect of also losing all that the two of them had built up over a decade and a half. He had to put his natural grieving process aside in order to conserve his energy for use in protecting his own future. In the end, Benjamin came out the loser as he had no legal position from which to argue. Through the solicitor he came to an agreement with the family that he would keep the contents of the flat and receive a quarter of the pension fund lump sum payment if he would give up any claims to the current and building society savings accounts. Benjamin and Rolf could have avoided the pain of this extended argument with the family if they had made their wishes clear by stating them in a will. Both men would have been protected, and if Rolf had wanted to make provision for his family, he could have said so. As it was, no one was sure what Rolf intended.

Wills can be made at any time during a person's life even when a person with AIDS is unwell and living in a hospice. If a will is made when the person is near death, a doctor will examine him or her and certify that he or she is of sound mind. Power of attorney, which appoints someone else to handle one's affairs on either a temporary or permanent basis, is important if the person with AIDS is experiencing dementia. Also, a living will which outlines care wishes in the event that the person with AIDS cannot express his or her wishes can be done at any time. Living wills are explained in detail in chapter 4 and are becoming more and more popular in the care of the terminally ill.

Perhaps one of the most complicated arguments over the estate of a person with AIDS to come our way is the case of Raoul and Dale. It is now nearly five years since Dale died, and there is still no resolution to the estate even though Raoul now has AIDS himself. The case has taken on similarities to Charles Dickens' *Bleak House*, and like the novel the proceeds of the estate may well be consumed in legal fees.

Raoul and Dale lived together for twenty years as servant and employer to family and to the public, but as lovers and partners in private. Dale was a wealthy, German stock market analyst with investments in off-shore banks, property around the world, and a great deal of both in the UK. His family, a brother and two sisters, lived in Germany and never visited him, although he would make yearly visits to his mother while she was still living. While he was visiting his family, he would send Raoul on expensive, first-class holidays to South America and then meet him for a reunion in the United States. He was a popular uncle and brother since he usually gave everyone expensive gifts or large sums of money when he visited Germany. This pattern continued for the twenty years of the relationship until Dale suddenly fell ill with pneumonia.

During Dale's first illness his brother flew over to visit and was introduced to Raoul as Dale's houseman. It was during Dale's final illness in the hospice that he began to acknowledge Raoul and his relationship. Dale made several wills during this time covering his property in different parts of the world and made financial provision for Raoul as well as assisting him to obtain a residence permit in the EC. The brother flew back for the funeral and began to realise that Raoul had been more than a servant and that he was the main beneficiary of Dale's will. A combination of anger, guilt and greed seems to be fuelling the family's relentless attempts to contest the will. Although Raoul has received some money from insurance policies, the major portion of the money and the property, both in the UK and abroad, is still awaiting settlement. Each side threatens the other with legal action and/or personal disclosure about the deceased's life; settlements are offered, agreed upon, and then broken; and the process continues over the years. The hospice has been involved as support for both the family and the partner and does not take sides in the legal action. However, the inter-disciplinary team do wonder if this is not a form of delayed bereavement and that both sides may be keeping the issue alive as a means of keeping Dale alive in their minds. All parties seem unwilling to relinquish the image of the man they know, and it is obvious that no one is really moving on with their lives.

This example demonstrates that the boundaries between practical issues and counselling issues are often blurred. It is often easy or convenient to solve practical issues of housing, welfare benefits, or after-death arrangement and these must be done; however, there is a constant interaction between these two areas. When working with PWAs, their surviving families, and partners, counsellors and pastors need to be especially sensitive to this phenomenon and not be misled into believing that practical issues can be separated from emotional needs.

7

STAFF ISSUES

James was a young man who desperately wanted to work in the field of HIV/AIDS counselling and had interviewed for several jobs without any success. After he was rejected for the third time for a hospice counselling job, he asked to speak with one of the selection panel in hopes of determining why he had been passed over. At the meeting James explained in detail his commitment to the work as well as his numerous qualifications and expressed frustration at being turned down yet again. The counsellor who he had come to see asked James why he wanted so badly to do this type of work.

In reply James snapped, 'I answered that in the interview, and I thought I made myself perfectly clear. I feel called to this kind of work and feel that I can make an important contribution. I'm not afraid of working with gay people or the terminally ill.'

During the ensuing discussion the counsellor was able to suggest that there might be more to his stated reasons than appeared at first view. James described himself as someone who gave 110 per cent to any job he took on and that his personal life was always centred around his work relationships. Although he was approaching thirty-five he had never maintained a long-term relationship with a woman but said he was sure that 'he would settle down' some day when he found 'the right girl'. When the counsellor brought up the issue of sexual identity James reacted with hostility and attempted to leave the room. After some calming words, he began to talk more freely about his feelings and confessed that he had left therapy because his therapist 'wanted to talk about sex all the time'. It was clear that James had a good deal of ambivalence about his sexual identity and that the

underlying reason for wanting to work in the field of HIV/
AIDS was an unstated desire to explore those feelings. The
counsellor suggested that the interview panels must have been
aware of those feelings either consciously or unconsciously.
James grudgingly accepted the recommendation that he go
back into therapy with a view of exploring these issues before
applying again for work in HIV/AIDS.

This situation was chosen to open the discussion of staff
issues because it illustrates the complex nature of the decision
to work in the field of HIV/AIDS. There are both stated and
unstated reasons for doing so, and it is important to understand them. Whether we are willing to admit it or not, it
seems almost impossible to come to this type of work without
an agenda. Some agendas can be good and can be the motivation for committed and quality work. On the other hand as
in James' case, if members of the interdisciplinary team are
not aware of their own agendas, problems in care delivery
and team co-operation can emerge.

The stated reasons for choosing to work in HIV/AIDS are
varied, but somewhat easier to discuss than the unstated.
Among the former can be a desire for professional development, a desire to work in a new challenging area, social/
political commitment, personal experience, and circumstance.
The list is not exhaustive, but in our experience they form
the main body of stated reasons for coming to AIDS hospice
work. The unstated reasons often centre on issues of sexuality, mortality/immortality questions, guilt, anger, and
Christian evangelism. As the unstated reasons are more discrete and less obvious they usually underlie the stated reasons.
The concern is for the patient who may be presented with
inappropriate working-out behaviours by people with unex-
plored reasons for working in HIV/AIDS. If one chooses to
work in HIV/AIDS caring situations, it inevitably affects
other areas of one's life. In the later section of this chapter
we will deal with the important issues of staff support, burn
out, longevity, the impact of failures and successes as significant aspects of staff care.

Many hospice staff members come to the work as a means
of expanding their professional expertise. Junior doctors and
nurses need to add the experience of HIV/AIDS to their

training programme as they will face it whether they choose to work in a hospital or a community practice. Hospice care gives them an opportunity for a year or eighteen months to gain important experience in an intensive manner. For other health care professionals, HIV/AIDS provides a new area in which to develop skills and procedures. Occupational therapy and physiotherapy have developed specific procedures designed for the needs of HIV/AIDS patients. For the caring professions the implications are that there is a need to develop expertise across the professional disciplines for dealing with HIV/AIDS.

Awareness and education courses are often the route through which men and women in the caring professions begin to consider full-time work in the field. Many of the most experienced HIV/AIDS workers found their way to the work through this route in the early 1980s, especially in counselling and pastoral care. The courses offered by Care and Resources for People Affected by HIV/AIDS (CARA), AIDS Care Education and Training (ACET), the Mildmay seminars on AIDS, the Terrence Higgins Trust, the London Lighthouse, and local health authority training programmes are responsible for bringing a number of people to the field.

Training and education courses have attracted people who enjoy the challenge of a new job which can offer the opportunity to create services and programmes. As mentioned in chapter 1, this was the motivating factor in Shirley's decision to enter the field of HIV/AIDS. It was the opportunity to join an institution at the beginning of its new life as an AIDS hospice and to set up the counselling and welfare department. The commitment to HIV/AIDS followed quickly through experience of day-to-day contact with patients and their families and partners. However, Shirley warns:

> There is a negative side to this motivation; it is easy to fall into the trap of always looking for a new challenge and not sticking to see the work through to maturity. At the same time, it is important to know when to move on and when to begin looking for someone with whom you can safely leave the work you've begun. Hopefully, management will acknowledge the individual's pro-

fessional development as an important aspect of the job and assist with career decisions.

There is more risk to accepting work in the area when seeking a new challenge than might be apparent at first glance. It is more than possible to find oneself taking up work which will involve a good deal of personal and professional risk. One AIDS hospice chaplain, the Revd Peter Clarke, speaks openly about his experience of coming to work in the field of HIV/AIDS. Peter left a career in the police to offer himself for full-time ministry in the Baptist denomination. After some years of successful and rewarding pastoral work, he was asked to consider becoming the chaplain to Mildmay AIDS Hospice. 'I had no idea what I was getting myself into, but I began to get some glimpse of what it might mean when I enrolled in the CARA training course for Christians working in HIV/AIDS. I have found that my preconceptions, beliefs, and attitudes have been challenged and have grown through the work with AIDS patients.' An important aspect of this growth has been the establishment of the ecumenical chaplaincy team which Peter developed in the hospice. Most clergy stay quite closely tied by denominational boundaries, and it was an enriching and maturing experience for Peter to work alongside Anglican, Jewish, Roman Catholic, Methodist, and Muslim colleagues. 'I've come to understand the variety and richness of religious experience which many patients bring to our life here at the hospice. At the same time I have deepened my own faith and my allegiance to the Baptist tradition.'

Some of the most productive and dynamic members of any interdisciplinary team are those who have come to work in HIV/AIDS because of a deeply held sense of social and/or political commitment. Early responses to the care needs of PWAs come from the gay community, the Terrence Higgins Trust most notably, and today gay men and women make up a large proportion of nurses, doctors, counsellors, clergy, and volunteers in hospitals, hospices and voluntary and statutory caring agencies. In the gay community there is often a feeling of responsibility to others due to the prejudice which is at large in society about sexual identity. In London alone there are over ten volunteer-based organisations providing care, counselling, housing, befriending, day centres, and many other services which have either come from or are staffed by the gay community. Another group whose response has been on both an individual and community level are Christians. The modern hospice movement was founded in England with a strong Christian component by Dame Cicely Saunders and that model has guided the development of AIDS hospices throughout the world. Jesus offers the model of a loving God who does not punish through infection, illness or disease. The Bishop of Monmouth, the Rt Revd Rowan Williams, affirmed this when he formulated a theological response to AIDS:

> The call of God that both challenges us and sets us free is to be heard in the voices of all who suffer; they are a major way in which God breaks open our self-possession or self-satisfaction or religiosity, and are in that sense . . . a means of grace for us, an occasion for deepening conversion. If we follow the example of Jesus, our response to each other's needs will be that of compassion and service not judgement.

This eloquent statement of Christian belief describes why so many Christians are found in the caring professions and particularly in HIV/AIDS.

While social and/or political commitment can be a positive motivation for working with PWAs it can also cause great difficulties. It is possible to allow one's underlying beliefs to become the overriding agenda, and this can result in inappropriate priorities. The PWA must always take precedence as a human being over any political, social, or religious commitment when considering care needs. The bedside of an ill or dying patient is not the place to exercise missionary zeal or political correctness.

Personal experience of HIV/AIDS has produced a growing number of people who have a desire to make a contribution to the care of PWAs. As it is one of the most delicate of reasons for entering the field, it is important that adequate time is given for grieving or acceptance of loss at several levels before taking up work in HIV/AIDS. The death of a son at an AIDS hospice in London brought Ellen to join a group in her local community who are working to establish a hospice. When Ellen's son, Peter, was ill and needed full-time nursing care which she could not provide she was appalled that they had to leave their home in the south of England and move him to London. Peter's care needs could no longer be met at home even with the provision of visiting community nurses, and there was no other alternative aside from acute-care centres in local hospitals. The strain this caused on the family was debilitating, and Ellen felt that no one should have to resort to such extreme measures. At the same time she was impressed with the level of personal attention given to both Peter and the family in a hospice setting, and she became convinced that this was something that should be available in all local communities. Her personal experience drew her to join with others in her area to found a hospice modelled on her personal experience.

As said earlier in this chapter, the unstated reasons for wanting to work in the area of HIV/AIDS are more discrete and often underlie the stated reasons. However, this does not make them less important, only more difficult to deal with and to identify. It is important that when interdisciplinary team staff members are being recruited that this important area is not overlooked. This discussion of unstated reasons is an attempt to make them more accessible for discussion and consideration. It also must be said that having unstated reasons for wanting to work in the field is not automatic grounds for refusal, but it is important that they be taken into consideration and balanced with other motivating factors. When this is done many staff problems can be avoided at a later date.

The most obvious unstated reasons are sexuality issues, and because of the ambivalent attitude our society projects about sexuality it is perhaps the most difficult to consider. The important point about sexual issues is that they can inhibit and confuse the work of staff members if they are not addressed. In AIDS hospice work many of the patients are gay and people will have strong feelings about this. In our experience many people who have ambivalent feelings about their own sexuality will be attracted to work in the field. They may or may not admit their ambivalence and feel at an unconscious level that they can deal with their ambivalence if they can associate with gay people in a safe controlled environment. In practice the opposite often happens, and we have seen strong reactions cutting both ways. The unconscious feeling that they can ask questions and explore may lead a staff member to confront powerful challenges to their overt sexual identity. This can result in disruption to care services and to new problems being introduced to people who are already quite vulnerable. Another common approach to dealing with sexual ambivalence within the AIDS hospice setting is that the hospice can become a place to avoid questions about sexuality. Like James in the opening example, prospective staff members may say quite strongly that they are not afraid of working with PWAs and feel that they can test and prove the strength of their sexual orientation by working in an AIDS hospice. An interesting example of this was with Roy who came to do a summer chaplaincy placement on an AIDS ward in a large New York hospital. Roy stated two things at the initial work supervision session: his brother was gay, and he was not. The other members of the chaplaincy team expressed their surprise that he felt he should introduce himself in that manner. Roy saw nothing odd about it and went on to say that he just wanted everyone to know 'where he was coming from'. The subsequent team meetings over the summer were dominated with Roy's inappropriate attachments to the patients on his ward, and he was disciplined for his behaviour on several occasions. As the summer drew to a close, the team was able to discern a pattern to Roy's relationships with the PWAs on his wards. An initial tentative visit to introduce himself was followed by twice daily pastoral visits. Then Roy would find himself deeply involved in the patient's personal life, even to the point of seeing the patient on a social basis when he was released from the hospital. Often this was followed by an abrupt breaking off of the friendship when in Roy's words, 'They always started getting the wrong idea about me'. Clearly he was using his entrée to vulnerable people to explore his own ambivalent sexuality even going to the extreme of participating in the gay person's personal life. When the situation got to be more than he could cope with he withdrew, leaving the

PWA with a new problem with which to deal. We cannot emphasise too strongly the potential for personal, professional, and institutional disaster brought to the field of HIV/AIDS by staff members with unstated sexual agendas.

The potential for personal pain and suffering is great also for those staff members who are carrying unstated agendas about mortality and immortality. It is accepted practice that anyone suffering from a major bereavement should avoid working with the terminally ill for at least a year. However, it is not always easy to define the meaning of a major bereavement or to determine how long the grieving process will take. It also must be said that many of the best people in the field have lost friends or partners to the illness and have focused their experience of loss into something positive by working with those who continue to live.

One of us experienced both sides of this unstated reason for coming to work in HIV/AIDS. A close friend of Alvin's died of AIDS while they were both at theological college. After a summer of grieving Alvin went to work as a chaplain's assistant in a cancer hospice in the north of England. All went well for the first week or so, but he found that he could not bring himself to enter a patient's room unless invited. The visits were usually short, and he left feeling that he had been of no use to the patient or family. Perhaps even more disturbing was what happened each time he came home from the hospice. The trip necessitated a long Metro ride from one side of the city to the other, and Alvin found himself feeling very sad as the journey ended, and by the time he reached his destination he was fighting to restrain tears for no obvious reason. The situation was brought to a head on the day that Alvin thought he saw his dead friend sitting across from him on the Metro, and he immediately went back to the hospice to speak with the chaplain. By surrounding himself with dying people, Alvin found himself on the sharp end of grieving. Obviously, for the best of reasons possible he was trying to do too much too soon and Alvin ended his placement. Two years later he became a volunteer at the Mildmay and has been able to negotiate his grief into a positive contribution to the care of PWAs.

Another aspect of the unstated mortality agenda is the

other side of the coin. It is not uncommon for people who have unresolved fears about death to want to work with the dying. In an odd way, they feel that they have taken control of mortality and have escaped the inevitability of their own death. 'If you keep running fast enough, you won't get caught.' This unstated agenda is often picked up by patients first as they are more sensitive to the staff member's omnipotence and will feel uncomfortable around them. On the other hand, some staff members will use working with the terminally ill as a means of coming to terms with their own death. This is not as harmful to the patient if the staff member can keep his or her own agenda emotionally distanced from work.

Guilt is a prime motivator in our society and those who come to work in a hospice setting are not exempt from being driven by the need to make up for something. This most often takes the form of feeling that they have not done enough for someone in their own life. In some situations we all feel, rightly or wrongly, that we could have done more for someone in pain or suffering from a long chronic illness. We may be carrying around guilt which is not associated with death and dying at all and find ourselves in the very demanding situation of hospice work. The caring professions are full of people who are not in touch with their own feelings of guilt and carry the burden throughout their daily life. These people often end up attacking the institution for not doing enough for the patients or not caring enough about patient needs. Staff meetings can become the stage upon which these feelings are acted out with the interdisciplinary team being divided into 'good' and 'bad' carers. In reality what they are saying to themselves unconsciously is that they did not care enough, and these punishing feelings are off-loaded onto the hospice or colleagues. The Ward Support Group at Mildmay AIDS Hospice was best attended when the ward experienced failures or successes, and at these times scapegoating of disciplines or staff were quite common; however, the disciplines would change from time to time. Now there is a review of the care plan after each patient leaves the hospice, so that issues of success and failure can be dealt with in a less threatening and more open manner. The potential for our guilty feelings to be triggered off is enormous and can result in anxiety attacks and eventual exhaustion and job burn-out.

Anger is another double-edged sword. As mentioned earlier many people will come to work in HIV/AIDS because they want to improve on the quality of care experienced previously, and these people are usually in touch with their anger as a motivating factor. On the other hand, many angry people don't realise they are angry. It is almost trite nowadays to say that depression is anger turned inside, but this is a helpful way of looking at it. As an unstated reason for wanting to work in a hospice setting, anger is a dangerous and volatile element, and one which needs to be looked at carefully. When the Mildmay Hospice opened and began to recruit volunteers they received over 260 applications for thirty positions as ward volunteers. This huge response was narrowed down to forty who were interviewed. A careful reading of the applications revealed that many of the applicants were very angry people, and this was affirmed when the hospice revealed several irate letters from those not chosen. The applicants were asked to write about their motivation for wanting to work in an AIDS hospice and about their personal experience of loss. These two questions, more than any other, seemed to allow people to express their frustrations and angry feelings about death, health care, AIDS, and many other topics. The destructive quality of anger is something which should not be unleashed on PWAs, or anyone who is ill for that matter.

One of the nursing staff in an AIDS hospice was a young woman who was seething with anger about almost every aspect of her life. Josephine only worked for a short time at the hospice, but in the few months she was there her anger caused an impressive amount of damage among staff and patients. She complained that there were not proper break facilities for the nursing staff which was true. Her distrust of the institution would not allow the hospice time to provide a space, and when one was provided it did not meet her standards. Her other complaints ranged from dissatisfaction with the duty rota to the level of cleaning done by the housekeepers. Her family background explained a good deal about her unstated feelings of anger. She was a person who was

103

both attracted and repelled by institutional life which modelled family life for her. As a lesbian living with a partner, her church hierarchy was uneasy about sending her forward for ordination and her family was not supportive of her lifestyle. She had made a life for herself as a nurse, but there was too much about health care institutions which resembled family life to her. In fact, there was little about the hospice which she found acceptable. When questioned about her feelings, she said, 'I knew this place wouldn't be all it promised to be. They're just a bunch of do gooders who want to get their hands on PWAs to make themselves feel good.' In staff meetings she was disruptive to the point of insubordination and eventually left to train for the ordained ministry. Her parting shot was a good example of unstated and misplaced anger. 'I only came here to fill in time before I went off to training college. I knew you couldn't trust a place like this and I was proved correct. It's all a fraud.' She was a person consumed by her own anger and the anger never allowed her to see the reality of the hospice, both the good and the bad. Her anger prevented her from seeing the caring and well-intentioned staff who were struggling to get a new institution on its feet.

This story would be sad enough if Josephine's anger only focused on the hospice, but unfortunately it affected the patients as well. Initially the hospice residents had a positive response to her, but eventually her negative attitude added an extra burden for them to shoulder at a time when they could ill afford it. At such an early stage in its life as a hospice, the institution was not equipped to handle Josephine's anger and needless to say it was a relief when she did leave.

Christians often are motivated by a commitment to the example of Jesus to serve the marginalised of society. Most Christians would see it as their duty to be involved in all aspects of life and not to separate themselves within an isolated self-referencing community. There is a long tradition of Christian work with the sick and dying, and the church is a major provider of health care, hospital, and hospice provision. In the field of HIV/AIDS such organisations as Care and Resources for People Affected by HIV/AIDS (CARA), Christians in Hackney AIDS Initiative (CHAI), AIDS Care

Education and Training (ACET), and Mildmay AIDS Hospice have a Christian foundation and are recognised leaders in the field.

However, there is another side to Christian commitment which brings people to the work, and it is not always acknowledged. Some Christians who come from a literalist tradition have extreme views concerning the nature of illness and the manner in which God works in the world. They would hold that one's behaviour is directly evaluated by God and then judged in this life. From this belief proceeds the idea that God punishes through illness, and while all mainstream Christians would deny this proposition it has been a factor in bringing people to work in HIV/AIDS. It is from this misguided interpretation of scripture that they take the idea that they must convert those whom they see as existing in a state of sin to their way of thinking. This is a type of theological thinking which has no place in the care of PWAs, and one which brings the church into disrepute. This unstated agenda can cause major problems in both the interdisciplinary team and with PWAs.

Usually people wanting to work in HIV/AIDS for this reason are easily identified at initial interviews if the interview panel asks simple and direct questions about what brings them to the field. However, this is not always the case. Clive applied to be a ward volunteer in an AIDS hospice and explained that it was his desire to serve God through caring for the ill. He was a member of his local church and was active in its many programmes. Initially he worked on the ward in a positive and co-operative manner, but within a short time the nurses on the ward began hearing complaints from patients. At first they just asked that Clive not visit them; then there were situations where Clive initiated conversations with hospice residents about the nature of God and the need to accept Jesus before being promised the continuance of God's love after death. The director of volunteers spoke with Clive and indicated that this kind of thing was not on. Clive agreed, but defended himself by saying that the patients had wanted to talk about their spirituality. Everything went well for a few more weeks before Clive began arriving at the hospice wearing badges with religious messages. Over the next few weeks the badges multiplied to the point that the hospice residents felt oppressed by Clive's presenting himself as a walking signboard. The final discussion with Clive ended with the hospice asking him to resign as a volunteer, and Clive agreed saying that the hospice was preventing him from exercising his call to be an evangelist.

This example illustrates how easy it is for unstated reasons to damage the work of care-giving agencies. Problems such as these can be sorted out at a much earlier stage if the right questions are asked and pursued in initial interviews and training. We cannot emphasise too strongly the savings in time, energy, and pain if comprehensive and thorough screening and interviewing of all prospective staff is standard practice.

Many of the issues surrounding staff support can be avoided by good practice which includes a clear understanding of the concept and provides a wide variety of support options. As has been emphasised staff support begins with selection but should also include attention to the work environment, staff levels and conditions of service. In-service training should emphasise the types of support available to staff and the ability to recognise the symptoms of stress.

In an earlier example Josephine focused some of her anger on the work environment, specifically the lack of proper 'coffee break' facilities. Hospice work often demands a high degree of concentration and working with a variety of disciplines on a team can make staff feel lost and undervalued. Something as simple as a clean, well-decorated work environment contributes to a positive attitude towards the work and the hospice residents. Most hospices have taken this on board and have designed their facilities according to the needs of their residents and staff. Much time and care was taken by the two major AIDS hospices in London to determine the needs of the two groups, and the result is a casual non-institutional and home-like environment with space for visitors and privacy. Not only do the patients feel relaxed and welcome, but the staff feel that the environment supports the ethos of interdisciplinary care. In addition staffing levels and conditions of service must be clearly stated and fairly implemented for the staff to feel valued. It is easy to lose sight of staff needs in hospice situations and forget that the work is demanding and draining as well as being creative and important.

Staff support is the flavour of the month in health care agencies, and there has been a proliferation of support options including staff support groups, staff counsellors, staff facilitators, and work consultants to name just a few. While all these are important provisions for staff it is just as important to begin with a basic understanding for the need for support when working in a demanding situation and how to make use of what is available. We have led several staff support groups, and it is our experience that there is great variance in their usefulness. Those groups which are able to use support options usually have a clear understanding of the symptoms of stress and what a support group can do to alleviate it. Stress, burn-out, feelings of failure, and a desire to leave the job are symptoms of the pressures felt by staff working with PWAs. Stress-related symptoms can take many forms and some of the key indicators of staff members experiencing stress can be observed at interdisciplinary team meetings. Some of the more common symptoms are meetings which focus on the frustration over failure to get results and complaints about the quality of the team's work. Staff members will display an inability to determine priorities, coming to meetings with diaries full of things for which they are not prepared while leaving a desk with an in-tray of things not done. These danger signals usually extend to home-life where staff members will find themselves not contributing to important domestic decisions and regularly coming home late. A feeling that life is no fun is common for people experiencing stress and they feel much too busy to take regular exericise or holidays. These symptoms often culminate in personality clashes with supervisors or subordinates at work and a reluctance to discuss problems at home.

This bleak picture of a staff under stress can be alleviated to a great degree by the variety of staff support options described earlier as 'flavour of the month'. The most common is a staff support group where team members can discuss the frustrations of the job as well as the successes rather than focusing on specific patients or cases. The focus here is on what the staff member is feeling about work and how work affects the wider picture of their life. Individual appointments with a staff counsellor can be useful when a particular problem needs to be discussed in depth. However, it is our experience that staff are reluctant to use a staff counsellor as it marks them a 'problem person'. The most immediate form of support available to most staff members is from the manager. This is an important managerial role and one which can contribute to a smoothly running team. Regular meetings with the manager to discuss such topics as work relations, career development, and feelings and attitudes about the job should be a significant part of a manager's job. A staff consultant can introduce the concepts of support to a staff and encourage them to widen their support networks to include not only work but also support by peers and colleagues, home, and community.

The authors cannot leave the discussion of staff support and staff issues without saying something about an often neglected aspect of staff life, namely humour. To those outside the world of HIV/AIDS and hospice work, it may seem like a serious and dark environment. Nothing could be farther from the truth. There is a great deal of living to be done in hospice situations by both residents and staff as well as their families, partners, and friends. When we do not split off the dying process from life, it is put into perspective and life continues to have value and joy. Humour is the grease which keeps the caring wheels turning when working with PWAs, and it is easy to forget that people do not lose their need for laughter when they are ill. Hospice life is full of celebration, parties, and the affirmation that life is good. Birthdays, baptisms, anniversaries, holidays, and even marriages are just a few of the joyful and humorous occasions lived out by the hospice caring community. We close this chapter with a story about the first Guy Fawkes celebration held at the Mildmay AIDS Hospice.

When the hospice first opened the glass conservatory which sits adjacent to Elizabeth Ward on the top floor did not exist. There was a large open space which was filled with tubs of flowers and garden furniture and was the setting for barbecues in good weather. Staff and volunteers suggested a traditional Guy Fawkes celebration with fireworks and food. Friends and family were invited and a crowd of about fifty people came along on the night. The volunteers had organised the fireworks, and we gathered on the roof to light them. Patients in wheelchairs, their families and friends joined with staff to watch a very creditable fireworks display which ended with everyone being given sparklers to light. Some of us took them inside to share with those who couldn't come outside. We were well into our sausages and jacket potatoes when the lights went out and the fire alarms blared out. No one panicked, but there was a good deal of tense discussion about what to do next. Soon fire engines were turning into the hospice forecourt, and the staff was busily trying to evacuate the ward. Everything was called to a halt when the chief explained to us that we had set off the alarm with our fireworks, most likely the sparklers brought into the hospice dayroom. Rather shamefacedly the over eager volunteers admitted it was their doing, and we regrouped to continue our Guy Fawkes celebration.

8

AIDS – THE CHANGING SCENE

How is it possible to conclude a book like this when the story of HIV/AIDS is still being written? Over the five years of the Mildmay's existence, we have moved from providing care predominantly for gay men, to haemophiliacs, women, and children, and now to a growing number of entire families. It is important that as HIV/AIDS moves into the wider community that care and counselling provisions are adapted to meet wider needs. The movement will be towards community-based care to support existing residential care. In the past five years, we have seen one out of every ten PWAs in England at Mildmay AIDS Hospice and base our thoughts about the future on our experience of the past.

In the past decade we have seen public knowledge and attitudes shift and change about HIV/AIDS from fear and lack of knowledge, to acceptance and understanding in many areas. Today we seem to be experiencing a time of complacency, and the fear is that the wider community are ignoring what they know about the HIV virus and about its transmission. We are seeing more young men who are presenting with AIDS-related illnesses from what appears to be a quite recent transmission of the HIV virus. Needless to say this is worrying. In this chapter we will discuss the HIV/AIDS scene as it presents itself at the time of writing as filtered through our experience in hospice work. It is useful to see where we have been and, hopefully, make some predictions about where we are going.

We are seeing more women, both African and Caucasian. AIDS hospices are no longer the exclusive enclaves of gay men. The growth in today's HIV/AIDS population appears to be coming through heterosexual transmission and drug use. This is important because as the HIV virus moves into the female population there is the possibility that children will be born HIV positive. Statistically a woman's life expectancy is significantly less than a man's when she is tested positive for HIV. One of the reasons for this is that women are not being tested until they present with an AIDS-related illness; this means they have not had the advantage of prophylactic treatments such as AZT and/or pentamidine. Also, many of the diseases affecting HIV positive women do not carry an AIDS diagnosis. This has profound care and counselling implications.

There has been a consistent growth in residential care provision. Mildmay AIDS Hospice began five years ago with one ward of nine beds and has moved to three wards and a total of twenty-eight beds and a day centre. There are further plans for a twelve-bedded family unit to be completed in 1993. AIDS-dedicated hospices have opened in other parts of the country, and this means that PWAs can now be treated and cared for in their local communities such as The Sanctuary in Bournemouth and Milestone Hospice in Edinburgh. The interdisciplinary approach to the terminal care of PWAs pioneered at Mildmay has become the standard of good practice accepted throughout the country and in Africa.

We are seeing more families. AIDS is beginning to move through families, both here and in the third world. AIDS is no longer only a gay man's problem and is affecting a wider spectrum of the population. Drug using families, as well as families with a history of haemophilia, are being affected. Babies are being infected with the HIV virus *in utero* and women have acquired the virus through heterosexual sex with drug-using or haemophiliac husbands. A large take up in the Mildmay Day Centre is from women and children.

The average age of the adult PWAs we see is dropping. This is disturbing for many reasons, but perhaps the main one is what this implies. HIV transmission must have taken place after the government's nationwide education projects had begun. The message may have been received by young people, but is it being listened to? At the same time many sexually transmitted disease clinics report an increase in the numbers of younger gay men who are presenting with

111

conditions other than HIV. What this appears to mean is that younger men and women are reacting against the idea of safer sex practices. If these early predictions are true indicators of new behaviour, the government and health care agencies will need to reinforce education programmes about the dangers of HIV transmission. The ACET group has done extensive work in this area and has produced some excellent teaching materials for primary and secondary schools. The churches are beginning to accept a need for teaching in this area, and recently the London Diocesan Board of Education has adopted guidelines for the teaching about HIV/AIDS as have Anglican dioceses in other parts of the country. Southwark Diocese was the first diocese to adopt a policy about HIV/AIDS, and many of the Christian-based AIDS caring agencies have educational components as part of their work. CARA offers a programme of speakers for higher education, and the Terrence Higgins Trust Roadshow is a well-known educational tool dealing with safer sex practices and information about HIV/AIDS. The information may be getting out to young people, but the next step appears to be developing ideas about changing behaviour.

People with AIDS are living longer. The news about HIV/AIDS is not all bad. We have developed better prophylactic treatments for AIDS-related illnesses, and people who survive their first serious illness have a much longer life expectancy. Testing is much more common and reliable today, and this has allowed people to take advantage of prophylactic drugs. One of the reasons that men have a longer life expectancy when diagnosed with AIDS is that they have usually been tested earlier than women. The area for development here is to convince women that early testing is called for if they suspect any possibilty of an HIV transmission. Another reason is that people are receiving more emotional and social support, and this may well contribute to longer life. This care most certainly contributes to better quality of life. Much of this support comes from the voluntary sector, and we question how much longer the government can rely on this response. The US experience is that after an initial ten-year period of positive response the voluntary sector suffered a decline. This was partially due to the number of workers declining as many became sick themselves from AIDS-related illnesses and partially from volunteer burn-out. Providing care for PWAs can be an emotionally draining experience, and we observe about a two-year life span for volunteers, nurses, and counsellors in the field. More counselling and pastoral care will be required as people live longer. As AIDS moves towards being a chronic disease, PWAs will need assistance in adjusting and making sense of lives limited by illness.

There is a definite move towards community-based care. There are some lessons we can learn from the North American experience and this may well be one of them. In the UK hospice provision is primarily residential while in the US the opposite is true. Hospice care teams which work from a centre and visit patients' homes to give health care, monitor pain relief, and co-ordinate care and counselling are the American model. Residential hospice care is very expensive, and we may have to look to adopting the US model in time. All hospices are now in the process of developing community-based care teams because it allows another dimension to patient choice. Patient choice and control are always perceived to be at a higher level by patients and their families when they are cared for at home. In practice, this is only partially true, and many patients mistake the feelings of alienation caused by entering residential care for loss of control. The AIDS hospice movement has attempted to combat this by providing a higher level of freedom of movement on a day-to-day basis determined by the patient's mobility, a more home-like environment in the facilities, and a wider variety of personal choice in determining daily routine. The government is putting new monies into community care, and this is obviously a growth area the Ministry of Health sees as important.

What are the implications for care if HIV/AIDS money within the NHS loses its ringfenced status? For the past five years AIDS funding has received priority status, and the funds for developing dedicated AIDS care units, research, and community care have been protected. We wonder how much longer this can continue. Already people are beginning to ask why AIDS money is ringfenced while money for other diseases is open to budget cuts. The facts are that many more women die of cervical cancer than AIDS-related illnesses and that the many forms of cancer are still much more prevalent than AIDS. Public pressure may cause the government to make changes. We mention this because should AIDS funding lose its protected status the voluntary agencies would be hard pressed to pick up more of the care needs than they are at present.

Adding to this problem is the fact that most acute-care centres have set up dedicated AIDS units rather than integrating the care of AIDS patients into general wards. In our opinion, PWAs should be cared for alongside all other patients; good nursing practice and hygiene prevent any danger of transmission. AIDS-related illnesses are just that, AIDS related. Many general hospices are accepting HIV/AIDS patients, and in the future there is hope that AIDS hospices will disappear. The development of hospices for PWAs was a response to a lack of hospice care anywhere else, not necessarily because of the unique nature of HIV/AIDS or the population in which it was initially encountered. It is good to keep this in mind.

The HIV/AIDS pandemic has reminded the church of its need to examine and to develop a theology of sexuality. Some church bodies in the US have used this opportunity to review their attitudes about sexuality which includes sexual behaviour, sexual orientation, and moral theology. Early on in the pandemic, fundamentalist Christians and Jews tied AIDS to judgement, but that type of thinking was quickly dismissed by all mainstream churches. What is needed is an open discussion of the issues surrounding sexuality. It is surprising that so little theological discussion of worth has resulted; the interesting work has been done in pastoral care.

At the beginning of this short chapter we asked a question concerning how to conclude a story that is still being written – the story of HIV/AIDS. The answer is that there is no conclusion for us as our involvement with PWAs continues on a daily basis. In our hearts we know that a time will come when the HIV virus and AIDS-related illnesses will be only a bad memory. We are both old enough to remember the spectre of polio in the late 1940s and 1950s and the fear, pain, and death which surrounded that disease. We feel that AIDS will be in that category someday; however, it may well not be in our lifetime. In many ways the title of this book summarises what AIDS has been for those of us involved in pastoral care and counselling, a time of growing up. Although we were mature adults when AIDS appeared in the early 1980s, sometimes we feel that we did not really begin to mature as human beings and as Christians until we found ourselves in the middle of the pandemic.

As we faced death after death, working with the survivors and then watching the survivors die, we have asked ourselves many times what good can come out of all this? The answer we have reached is twofold. For ourselves, we have grown up as Christians through the love and courage we have seen modelled in the AIDS caring community. We have seen that love pass throughout the group, now known as people living with AIDS, without any extinguishing of joy or hope, and that experience has helped us to understand in a very deep way the gospel imperative to love one another. Faced with AIDS we have little else to offer, and as God has taught us through the life of Jesus that is more than enough. The other good we see coming from living the past decade with AIDS is an affirmation of the indomitable spirit of hope bred into humankind. It is easy, and sometimes convenient, to believe that we are the masters of our world, and it takes something like AIDS to make us realise how much there is yet to know, about both the physical and spiritual world. The confidence and courage that many of the people with whom we have worked have faced AIDS makes us hopeful for the future.

Hospice work affirms the hope for today and the present, that the quality of life is important until the last breath, as well as pointing us toward what lies ahead. For that we thank Paul, Tim, Sarah, Michael, Schabel, Raoul, Stephen, Scottie, Regina, Agatha, Ellen, Peter, Josephine, Roy, Gary, Paul, Terry, Graeme, Leila, Mark, Melanie, Ralph, Jason, Robert, and all the others we have known for allowing us to grow up in such a place with you.

115

SUGGESTED READING

Ainsworth-Smith, Ian, and P. Speck. *Letting Go*, SPCK, 1982.

Altman, Dennis. *AIDS and The New Puritanism*, Pluto Press, 1986.

Bennets, Chris, M. Brown and J. Sloan. *AIDS: The Hidden Agenda in Child Sexual Abuse*, Longman Group UK, 1992.

Cassidy, Sheila. *Sharing the Darkness: The Spirituality of Caring*, Darton, Longman and Todd, 1988.

Crowther, Colin E. *AIDS, A Christian Handbook*, Epworth Press, 1991.

Claxton, Rosie, and Tony Harrison. *Caring for Children with HIV and AIDS*, Edward Arnold, 1990.

Dixon, Patrick. *The Truth About Aids*, Kingsway, 1987.

Dominian, Jack. *Sexual Integrity: The Answer to AIDS*, Darton, Longman and Todd, 1987.

Fee, Elizabeth, and D. Fox, editors. *AIDS, The Burdens of History*, Berkeley, California, University of California Press Ltd, 1988.

Fortunato, John. *AIDS, The Spiritual Dilemma*, San Francisco, California, Harper and Row, 1987.

Foskett, John, and D. Lyall. *Helping the Helpers – Supervision and Pastoral Care*, SPCK, 1988.

Green, J. *Counselling in HIV Infection & Aids*, Oxford, Blackwell Scientific Publications, 1989.

Kirkpatrick, Bill. *AIDS: Sharing the Pain*, Darton, Longman and Todd, 1993.

Kubler-Ross, E. *AIDS, The Ultimate Challenge*, Basingstoke, Macmillan, 1987.